PROFILES

Bill Gates

Mark Zuckerberg

Steve Jobs

TECH TITANS

Sergey Brin

Larry Page

Jeff Bezos

ONE FRONTIER SIX BIOS

SCHOLASTIC INC.

New York   Toronto   London   Auckland
Sydney   Mexico City   New Delhi   Hong Kong

....

CONTENTS

INTRODUCTION

A FEW DEVELOPMENTS OVER THE CENTURIES, like the printing press, telegraph, radio, and television, have made titanic-sized changes in the way people share information. Each new development was a revolutionary improvement over the one before it. But perhaps the biggest technological leap of all has taken place with the creation of the computer. Computers have allowed information to be processed, used, and shared in ways it never had been before.

Like most technology, improvements in computers came slowly through the years. Then, in the 1970s, a new generation of computer whiz kids entered the scene. From that point on, one brilliant programmer after another has come up with innovative ways to use computers.

The six men featured in this book have changed computing forever. Each of them built on the technology that was available to him. Each of them created something new and exciting. Each of them has changed the way we live today. Bill Gates was instrumental in bringing computers into the homes and offices of the general public. The beautifully designed products of Steve Jobs have successfully put computers in our phones. Jeff Bezos has not only changed how we buy books, but in some cases how we read them, too. Sergey Brin and Larry Page have made it possible to find the answer to almost any question in seconds, with just a few keystrokes. Mark Zuckerberg has changed the way we socialize and stay connected with our friends.

Computers are part of everyday life for many people. On any given day, we may use our computers to find directions to a location, order a book or even a pizza, research a project and write a paper for school, play a video game, send messages to our friends (whether they live next door or on the other side of the globe), or share photographs and videos with the world.

Today, because of the groundbreaking work of these men, information of every kind is available at all times. Never before have so many facts and so much knowledge been at our fingertips. These six men are modern technology titans.

BILL GATES

BILL GATES is a computer programmer and businessman. He is best known for cofounding Microsoft, the world's largest personal-computer software company.

GATES MEETS THE WORLD

William Henry Gates III was born on October 28, 1955. He was named after his father, William Henry Gates II. To avoid confusion, the family called the boy Trey. Today Trey is better known as Bill Gates. Gates was the second child in the family, joining his older sister, Kristianne (Kristi). Gates's father was a lawyer. His mother, Mary Maxwell Gates, had been a schoolteacher before her son was born. Even after Gates's younger sister, Elizabeth (Libby), was born, their mother continued to be actively involved in various community and business projects.

At the family dinner table, Gates's parents discussed the latest business or volunteer efforts in which they were involved with their children. They encouraged their three kids to ask questions. The close-knit family spent a lot of time together and enjoyed working on puzzles and playing competitive trivia and card games. It was a lot of fun for all of them, but each member of the Gates family took games seriously because winning was important to each of them.

As Bill Gates grew up, he was curious about everything. He read the *World Book* encyclopedia in alphabetical order just for fun. He was shy, but he excelled academically at math and reading. His parents insisted that Gates get out of his comfort zone by participating in things he was not so good at, like football and soccer.

A CHALLENGING KID

Gates had an intense personality and a tendency to challenge his parents. By the time he was almost out of elementary school, he often ignored his mother's wishes that he clean his bedroom and come to dinner. He was so disagreeable and stubborn that his parents were concerned. It seemed their son fought them over everything.

Since Gates had become difficult to handle, his parents decided to send him to a professional counselor. He went to that counselor for about a year. Gates would later recall that the counselor helped him understand there was no benefit to fighting with his parents, and that they were on his side no matter what. After this realization, Gates was more agreeable and things seemed to smooth out for the family.

When the time came to attend junior high, Gates's parents became concerned about him again. They wondered how he would do at a large public school. He was short and thin for his age, and he was still very shy. Another of their concerns was that Bill needed to go to a school that would satisfy his intelligence and curiosity. They decided to enroll him at Lakeside, an elite private school.

GATES MEETS A COMPUTER

Bill Gates entered seventh grade at Lakeside. At first he didn't like their strict rules, like wearing a jacket and tie, calling the teachers "master" and going to chapel every morning. But soon he found some friends who shared his interests in business and computer companies.

Then something happened at Lakeside School that changed his life.

The Mother's Club had a garage sale. From the proceeds, they rented a Teletype terminal that was connected to a computer at the University of Washington. They also purchased some computer time for the Lakeside students to use. At this time, in 1968, Teletype terminals

Keyboard for a Teletype computer.

were connected by phone lines to a mainframe computer in another location. The mainframe was a huge computer powerful enough to run many programs simultaneously.

When the new teletype computer terminal was installed at Lakeside, there was one big problem. The teachers didn't know how to work it or what do with it. They allowed students like Gates, who were eager to work with the computer, the freedom to figure it out by using it. Gates took the manuals home and studied them. Ultimately, he, his friend Paul Allen, and a few other students became the school's computer experts. By the time he was in the eighth grade—and way ahead in math—he was excused from math class to work on the computer.

Gates was amazed by what the computer could do. After working with it for a few months, he wrote his first software program. It was a tic-tac-toe game. He was fascinated by the fact that when he programmed software he would have instant results—the program would either work perfectly or it would fail. He dreamed that someday individuals would be able to have computers of their own. Gates would later say, "I'm sure that one reason I was so determined to help develop the personal computer is that I wanted one for myself."

Gates and his friends quickly used up all the prepaid time the Lakeside Mother's Club bought for them, and they wanted more—a lot more. Gates had to figure out how to pay for his own computer time. Gates and Allen found a local company that allowed them to have free computer time in exchange for finding problems with their computer software. They worked there mostly at night. Sometimes after his parents went to bed, Gates would sneak out of the house and go back to the computer center to use the computer all night long. Along the way, he learned everything he could about computers and studied every computer manual he could get his hands on.

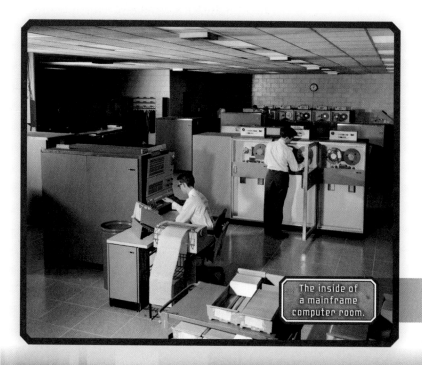

The inside of a mainframe computer room.

By the time he was in high school, the cost to access a mainframe computer was $40 per hour. To make money to pay for computer time, Gates and Allen got jobs as entry-level software programmers. During the summer, Gates and Allen were paid about $5,000 each, part of it in cash and part of it in computer time.

Even though he was still a student, Lakeside asked Gates, to write a software program that could be used to schedule students for classes. Since he wrote the program, he arranged it so he would be one of the few guys in a class full of girls. But even this edge didn't seem to help him in some social situations—the first girl he asked to the prom turned him down.

GATES IN CHARGE

Gates and his computer buddies became known as the Lakeside Programmers Group. Sometimes the group had arguments. Paul Allen was three years older than Gates, and the two of them struggled over who would have control. After one disagreement, Gates left the group. But Allen soon realized they needed him back, to do the programming. Gates agreed to return to the group under one condition, saying, "Look, if you want me to come back, you have to let me be in charge. But this is a dangerous thing, because if you put me in charge this time, I'm going to want to be in charge forever after." And from that point on, Gates was the boss.

Gates and Allen remained friends even after Allen graduated from high school. During the summer of 1972, an article appeared in *Electronics* magazine that caught the attention of sixteen-year-old Gates and nineteen-year-old Allen. It announced that a new company named Intel had released the 8008—a microprocessor computer chip (the command center of a computer). The 8008 was only capable of a few simple functions. But the teenagers wondered if they could program the Intel computer chip to do more than that.

Gates and Allen, in 1983, still friends.

By this time, Allen was attending college at Washington State University. Gates rode the bus back and forth across the state from Seattle to Pullman to visit Allen, and used the time to write a new software program to run on the 8008 Intel chip. The program was designed to collect data on the number of cars that drove down a particular street, and process the information into reports. If successful, it would be a way to make some money from his programming skills. Gates and Allen called the program Traf-O-Data.

They got the program to work, and Gates convinced some employees of the city of Seattle to come to his house so he could demonstrate it. When the moment arrived to demonstrate Traf-O-Data—the program didn't run correctly. Gates ran into the kitchen and insisted that his mom tell them that the program really did work. Although they didn't make a sale that night, Gates and Allen worked out the programming problems, and eventually made some money from it.

HARVARD BOUND

In 1973 Bill Gates graduated from high school and enrolled at Harvard University. Gates wasn't sure what he wanted to choose for his future career, but considered becoming a lawyer or a mathematician.

Gates had the tendency to attend classes in which he

was not enrolled, and skip the classes in which he was enrolled. This left him with free time, which he filled playing poker with his friends. To make it interesting for himself as the end of the semester approached, Gates would cram for his finals. He probably considered it a challenge to see how high a grade he could get with a minimum amount of effort.

Harvard University

At the time, Allen was working in nearby Boston as a computer programmer. This allowed the two of them to work together on different projects. In the spring of 1974, Intel announced the release of another major computer chip improvement. Their new microprocessor chip, the 8080, was ten times more powerful than the one before it—the chip inside the Traf-O-Data machine. Gates and Allen understood that this computer chip would change everything. The 8080 Intel computer chip was tiny, powerful, and reasonably priced (less than $200). It was clear to the two young men that this chip meant it would no longer be necessary to pay an hourly rate to gain access to a giant mainframe computer. The massive machines would become outdated. They would be replaced by a machine that would be smaller, more affordable, and more adaptable. They would be replaced by personal computers. Allen encouraged Gates to join him to start a company to build computer systems using the 8080 Intel chips. But Gates's parents wanted him to stay in college, so he did.

Months later, in January 1975, Gates and Allen were walking through Harvard Square when they saw the cover of *Popular Electronics*. The cover of the magazine announced a new computer called the Altair 8800 that contained the newest Intel microprocessor chip. It was being

Altair 8800 computer

sold as a kit for $397. It was sort of like getting both good news and bad news. The next generation of computers, personal computers, was on its way just like they thought. But they were horrified that someone else was doing what they wanted to do and feared their chance may be slipping away.

Gates and Allen realized the Altair 8800 did not have software, so it could not be programmed to do anything. Personal computers would need software to make them usable—and Gates knew he could supply it. Gates had never seen the Altair 8800 or the Intel microprocessor chip inside it, but he was determined that he could write software for it.

MICROSOFT IS BORN

Gates went to work in his Harvard dorm room. He began with BASIC (Beginner's All-Purpose Symbolic Instruction

Microsoft logo

Code), a computer programming code that had been in use since the mid-1960s. As he focused on writing the programming code, Gates rocked back and forth—something he'd done all of his life while deep in thought. He ignored all distractions and didn't see anyone. He lost track of time. Some days he didn't eat. He rarely slept and it was only when exhaustion overtook him that he would crash at his desk or on the floor. Finally, after five weeks of intense work, his software code was finished. Gates would later recall this period of time and say, "the world's first microcomputer software company was born. In time we'd name it 'Microsoft.'"

Gates and Allen knew the moment had come. To succeed in the computer software business, they had to jump in at the beginning. If they hesitated, the opportunity would pass them by. By the spring of 1975, Allen quit his job and nineteen-year-old Gates told his parents he wanted to take a leave from Harvard to start a software business. He promised them he would go back later to get a degree. They were disappointed that their son wanted to leave college, but they supported his decision. Gates said, "Getting in on the first stages of the PC revolution looked like the opportunity of a lifetime, and we seized it."

Allen and Gates moved with their brand-new business, Microsoft, to Albuquerque, New Mexico, in 1975. They had one goal in mind: "A computer on every desk and in every home." As their company grew, Microsoft wrote most of the BASIC programming software for companies like Apple, Commodore, and Radio Shack that sold personal computers to the public.

During the early years of Microsoft, Gates was writing programming code, but he also did most of the sales, finance, and

Microsoft cofounder, Gates, working on a computer.

marketing. He was just barely out of his teenage years, and was intimidated by it all. But in spite of that, he worked out deals with various companies so that each personal computer they sold would come with Microsoft software. These companies would pay Microsoft a royalty (percent of sales) for their software. At first Microsoft wrote different software programs to fit the needs of each company's machine. Over time, almost every computer sold had various Microsoft programs preinstalled.

MICROSOFT ON THE MOVE

By 1979 Gates and Allen moved Microsoft to a suburb of Seattle, Washington. The personal computer industry was gaining momentum and Microsoft had grown by leaps and bounds. By the next year, IBM planned to create a new line of personal computers and asked Microsoft to design a new operating system for it. An operating system controls and directs all the other software programs on a computer so they all work together— sort of like a policeman directing traffic at a busy intersection. Microsoft created the Microsoft Disc Operating System (MS-DOS), which became the operating system used in many early personal computers.

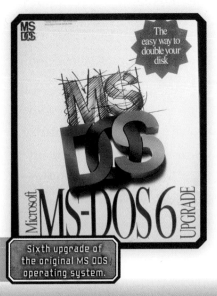

The easy way to double your disk

Sixth upgrade of the original MS DOS operating system.

As more and more computers using MS-DOS were sold, programmers all over the country began to develop software applications like word processing and spreadsheets to work with Microsoft's operating system. As these new application programs became available, computers were able to do more things.

Gates constantly looked for ways to improve Microsoft's software products. At the time, MS-DOS functioned by typing text into a blank screen. Bill Gates thought the next step should be a graphical operating system. He knew that using picture graphics would be easier for most people than typing in commands on a screen. Years before, an innovative computer engineer at the Stanford Research Institute, Doug Engelbart, invented the "mouse," which was issued a patent in 1970. The mouse could be used to point to and choose an object on a computer screen. In 1983 Microsoft incorporated the mouse with their new operating system based on pictures. They announced plans to release a new product

Gates with newly packaged Microsoft Word and Microsoft Mouse.

Gates's wife, Melinda French.

called Windows. At the same time, Apple Computer was also working on a graphical operating system. Steve Jobs, Apple's cofounder, approached Bill Gates to create the software for the Macintosh, their new computer. Gates worked with Jobs to create versions of Microsoft Word and Microsoft Excel for the Mac.

GATES BUILDS A FAMILY

As the years went by, Microsoft grew and flourished under the leadership of Bill Gates. By 1993 his thoughts turned toward his personal life. He became engaged to Melinda French, a young woman who worked at Microsoft. On January 1, 1994, they married in Hawaii. Sadly, later that year, Gates's mother died from cancer. Eventually, Bill and Melinda Gates went on to have three children: two daughters (Jennifer and Phoebe) and one son (Rory).

It seems that Bill Gates has always been able to predict what would happen next in the world of computers. Long before the Internet became part of our daily lives, Gates knew the next giant step would be to link computers together in order to exchange information between them. Like the interstate highway system, which allows traffic to move easily across the United States, the Internet, which in the early days was sometimes called the information superhighway, would allow information to move easily around the globe. Early on, Gates understood that this global connection of computers

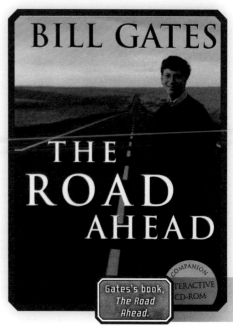

Gates's book, *The Road Ahead*.

would be more like a marketplace than a highway.

Gates and a few others were the pioneers of the computer industry, but Gates realized the next generation of whiz kids was on its way up. In his 1995 book, *The Road Ahead*, Gates wrote, "I know that as I write this there's at least one young person out there who will create a major new company, convinced that his or her insight into the communications revolution is the right one." He was right. When his book was released, Larry Page and Sergey Brin, the creators of Google, were twenty-two years old. Mark Zuckerberg, creator of Facebook, was eleven.

Gates at Harvard Commencement.

GATES GOES BACK TO SCHOOL, FOR A DAY

Even as Bill Gates divided his time between running Microsoft and his family, he never forgot the promise he'd made to his parents years earlier. When he wanted to take a leave of absence from Harvard, his parents worried he would never graduate. On June 7, 2007, Bill Gates was back at Harvard. Not to return as a student, but to give the commencement address and to receive an honorary degree. He ended his speech on a personal note. Gates looked at his father and said, "I've been waiting more than thirty years to say this. Dad, I always told you I'd come back and get my degree."

GIVING IT AWAY

Microsoft's success has made Bill Gates the richest man in America, with a current worth of approximately $56 billion. His great wealth prompted Gates to create a charitable organization called the Bill & Melinda Gates Foundation. At the end of June 2008, Bill Gates gave up day-to-day control of Microsoft in order to spend more time working with the foundation. Today Bill Gates works as hard for his charity as he once did to create Microsoft.

Gates is focused on improving education in America. The Gates Foundation funds computers, software, and Internet connectivity to some public libraries in order to provide Internet access to their communities. The foundation also

Gates and his wife, Melinda, speaking on behalf of their foundation at the International Aids Conference.

helps students get ready for college and awards many scholarships.

Another focus of the Gates Foundation is the fight against poor health in developing countries around the world. They work to make vaccines available in these areas—hoping that someday they will be able to completely eradicate diseases like polio.

Through the years, the Gates Foundation has given away millions of dollars to charitable causes. In June 2010 Bill and Melinda Gates took their giving to an even higher level. They and their friend Warren Buffett announced they had formed what they called the Giving Pledge. Gates promised to give away more than half of his money to charity in an effort to help solve some of society's problems. The Gates family believes that because they have been fortunate, they have a responsibility to use it to help others.

Gates and Buffett hoped they could convince other billionaires to follow their lead—and many have. As of April 2011, sixty-nine of America's richest families have publicly made the Giving Pledge to give the majority of their wealth to charity. Ultimately, these pledges will amount to hundreds of billions of dollars. The pledge is a moral commitment, not a legal one. Each family will choose how much money they will give and to whom they will give it. Since the interests of each family are different, a variety of charitable causes will be supported including medical research, health care, education, disadvantaged children, homelessness, substance abuse, and ministry.

Bill Gates grew up with a lot of advantages—he had a loving family, had an excellent education, and was intellectually gifted. One more advantage would influence his future success—at an early age, Gates had access to a computer when they were just beginning to be used by the public. Early on, he dreamed that someday nearly every office and home would have a personal computer—and because of Bill Gates, that dream has become a reality.

STEVE JOBS

STEVE JOBS was the cofounder of Apple Computer. He was the creative force behind popular products like the Mac computer, iPhone, iPad, and iPod.

ADOPTED

Joanne Carole Schieble was a pregnant, unmarried college student. She decided to place her child up for adoption—on one condition. The adoptive parents must be college graduates. The right adoptive parents were found—a lawyer and his wife. On February 24, 1955, Schieble's son was born in San Francisco. The adoption agency called the childless couple to tell them their child had arrived. But when they heard the baby was a boy, they decided not to take him— they wanted a girl instead.

Many families were on the waiting list to adopt a baby, so the agency called the next couple on the list, Paul and Clara Jobs. They were thrilled at the chance to adopt a newborn son. But there was a problem. Schieble found out that Clara had not graduated from college, and Paul had never graduated from high school. Since she wanted her son's parents to be college educated, at first she refused to sign the adoption papers. Finally, she agreed to let Clara and Paul Jobs adopt the boy—but only after they promised her they would send him to college. They brought their new son home and named him Steven Paul Jobs. Two years later, they adopted a daughter named Patty, who completed their family.

Steve Jobs's father was a machinist who enjoyed working on projects in his garage. When Jobs was about five years old, his father cleared off a section of his workbench so his son could have his own space for projects. He gave him some tools and showed him how to use them. Paul, who had learned about electronics by working on cars, spent a lot of time showing Steve how to take things apart and put them back together. By this time, the Jobs family lived in Mountain View, California, an area of the state where many engineers lived (this area would later be known as Silicon Valley). Paul Jobs taught his son the basics of how electronics worked.

One day a man named Larry Lang moved into the neighborhood. Lang worked as an engineer at Hewlett-Packard (HP), a major company that produced electronic

Present day Silicon Valley

products. He also tinkered on projects in his garage and left the garage door open, which let the kids in the area see what he was working on. He allowed young Steve Jobs to play with a microphone, battery, and speaker he had. Jobs wanted to learn more. Lang taught him how electronics were built and how they worked. This knowledge made a deep impact on Jobs. It allowed him to understand that electronics were not mysterious, magical things—they were built by regular people.

BAD BOY IN CLASS

Jobs was a very smart boy. His mother taught him to read before he was old enough to attend school. When he arrived at school, all he wanted to do was read books and chase butterflies. After the freedoms he'd had at home, he did not like the structure of school or the authority he encountered there.

By the time he was in third grade, Jobs still didn't like school. His reaction was to cause trouble. Jobs and his friend Rick Farentino set off explosives in the teacher's desk and let snakes loose in the classroom. Next they masterminded a plan. Step one: Approach their fellow students one by one and innocently ask for the combinations on their bicycle locks. Step two: Go to the bike rack at school and take each lock off of one bicycle and put it on a different one. Step three: Watch the mayhem. To their delight, it took until ten o'clock that night to get all the bicycles unlocked and returned to their rightful owners.

Jobs and Farentino built a reputation at school as troublemakers. It became clear to the school administration that the two boys should never be in the same classroom again. In fourth grade, they planned to separate them. One brave teacher, Imogene "Teddy" Hill, offered to take one of the boys in her advanced class. She happened to get Steve Jobs.

Mrs. Hill watched Jobs closely for about two weeks. Then one day she approached him with a humongous lollipop in her hand. She offered the young troublemaker a deal: If he took home a math workbook, did the work himself, and correctly answered at least 80 percent of the problems, then she would give him the lollipop and $5.

Jobs was so motivated by her offer that he took the math book home to work—and soon earned the candy and the money. She continued to encourage him with extra projects like a camera-making kit, with which he made his own lens and built a camera. He respected Mrs. Hill, and being in her class made him want to learn. Jobs would later say, "I'm 100% sure that if it hadn't been for Mrs. Hill in the fourth grade and a few others, I absolutely would have ended up in jail." Academically he made such progress in her class that the school system suggested he skip several grades. His parents allowed him to skip fifth grade, but no more.

Jobs went to Mountain View's Crittenden Middle School. Because he skipped the fifth grade, he was younger than everyone else. The rough-and-tumble school was the scene of frequent fights. Jobs hated it. One day when Jobs was in the seventh grade, he told his parents that he would never go back. His parents knew how determined and stubborn their son was. They knew he meant what he said, so they decided to move to the nearby city of Los Altos.

Garage in Los Altos—birthplace of Apple computer.

LOVE AT FIRST SIGHT

Jobs's interest in electronics continued to grow. His old neighbor, Larry Lang, had suggested to Steve that he become a member of Hewlett-Packard's Explorers Club. The organization allowed a group of kids to meet in the company cafeteria where employees would show them the company's latest projects. Steve soaked in everything he saw and heard. It was at HP that he saw a computer close-up for the first time. He fell in love with it.

One of HP's first personal computers, circa 1978.

About the same time, Jobs became friends with Bill Fernandez, who shared his interest in electronics. The garage at the Fernandez house became their hangout. Soon Fernandez introduced Jobs to one of his friends who lived down the street. Everyone called him Woz, but his name was Steve Wozniak. Woz, who was five years older than they were, was already a gifted programmer and knew much more about electronics than Jobs or Fernandez did.

Thirteen-year-old Jobs decided to build a frequency counter (an instrument that measures the number of electronic pulses during a specific period of time.) He realized he didn't have the parts he needed, or the money to buy them. But he knew where he could get them: Hewlett-Packard. He was not afraid to pursue what he wanted. And he wanted those parts. He looked in the local phone book and found the telephone number for Bill Hewlett, one of the owners of HP. Jobs called Hewlett on the phone and told him about his project and asked him for the parts he needed. Hewlett must have been impressed with Jobs's guts and intelligence. He sent Jobs the parts he wanted—and he gave him a summer job at HP. This might have been the first time Jobs fearlessly went after what he wanted, but it wouldn't be the last.

FULFILLING THE PROMISE OF COLLEGE

After Jobs graduated from high school, he told his parents the only college he wanted to attend was Reed College in Portland, Oregon. It was an excellent school, but it was very expensive. Remembering their promise to his birth mother that they would send him to college, Paul and Clara Jobs agreed. They paid his first year's tuition from their savings.

Jobs was a college student at Reed for about six months when he realized he didn't know what he wanted to do with

Reed College, Portland, Oregon.

his life. And he didn't think college would help him figure it out. Jobs also thought about the fact that he was spending money his hardworking parents had saved all their lives. He decided to quit college.

As soon as he made the decision to quit school, he dropped out of his required classes. But he began to sit in on classes that interested him—like calligraphy. Since he was no longer an official student at Reed College, he slept on the floor of a friend's dorm room.

At Reed, Jobs turned his attention to Eastern religions. He didn't have any money for food, so he collected soda bottles and returned them for the five-cent deposit. Since he had no money, once a week Jobs walked seven miles to the Hare Krishna temple for a meal. He became a vegetarian and began spending time working at an apple orchard called All-One Farm. To some of his friends, it seemed Jobs was searching for something. One of his college buddies, Dan Kottke, said, "I think it's clear that Steve always had a kind of chip on his shoulder. At some deep level, there was an insecurity that Steve had to go out and prove himself."

SEEKING WORK AND ENLIGHTENMENT

In 1974 nineteen-year-old Steve Jobs made his way back home to his parents. He looked for a job and answered an advertisement at Atari (maker of the Pong game). He had an interview with Al Alcorn, Atari's chief engineer. When he arrived at the interview, Alcorn saw that Jobs

The Atari 2600 video game console

was shabbily dressed and looked to him like a hippie. When the interview was over, Jobs once again showed his fearless determination when he refused to leave the office until Atari hired him. Alcorn saw Jobs's determination—and he saw something special about the young man, despite his appearance. Alcorn hired Jobs to work the night shift at Atari.

Jobs's interest in Hinduism deepened. He hadn't been at Atari very long when he decided to travel to India to meet Hindu gurus (teachers) hoping to find spiritual enlightenment. He convinced his friend Dan Kottke to go with him. At the time, Atari was having problems with their products in Germany. Alcorn agreed to pay for the trip—if Jobs first stopped over in Germany to fix their issues. When Jobs got to Germany, he corrected the problem in two hours, then continued on his way.

When he arrived in India, Jobs traded his T-shirt and jeans for traditional Indian clothing. For about a month, Jobs and Kottke traveled through India on foot. But Jobs didn't seem to find what he was looking for. After returning home, he continued his interest in Eastern religions and studied meditation and Zen Buddhism. When he arrived back at Atari to work, he had a shaved head and wore an Indian robe.

THE TWO STEVES GO INTO BUSINESS

Not long after his return, Jobs saw the cover of *Popular Electronics*. It was the issue that featured the Altair 8800 kit that contained the newest Intel microprocessor chip. At the same time Jobs read this magazine on the West Coast, Bill Gates was reading it on the East Coast. The same article would have a big impact on both their lives.

Jobs, his friend Woz, and other computer enthusiasts in the area attended a group meeting called the Homebrew Computer Club. They met to discuss computers and the latest developments. About a year after the Altair 8800 appeared on the cover of the magazine, Wozniak had designed a new circuit board for a computer. It was so innovative that Jobs suggested the two of them should go into business to sell it.

The two of them figured it would cost about $1,000 to buy the needed materials to build some circuit boards to sell. They didn't have that kind of money. And even if they could get it, they were not sure if they could ever sell enough circuit boards to make back the $1,000. Finally Jobs told Wozniak they should do it, because even if they failed they could always look back and know that they had once had a company of their own. To get the money for the parts they needed, Jobs sold his Volkswagen van and Wozniak sold his top-of-the-line HP programmable calculator.

SHINY NEW APPLE

After deciding to start a company, they had to name it. They thought about all sorts of technical-sounding names, but nothing seemed right. Finally Jobs suggested Apple— both because he loved the apple orchard at All-One Farm and because he was a fan of the Beatles, whose record label was Apple Records.

It was settled. Apple Computer was officially established in April 1976.

Their company headquarters was located in the garage of Jobs's parents' home. Wozniak worked on technical issues like designing and building the computer's circuit board. Jobs designed a wooden case for the circuit board. He also worked on the business side of things like getting parts, and began selling the finished product. They named their computer the Apple I.

On Labor Day 1976 Jobs and Wozniak took Apple I to the personal computer festival in Atlantic City, New Jersey. At the trade show, the major computer companies had fancy booths and expensive promotional materials. In sharp contrast, the Apple Computer booth had a card table, Steve

Apple I computer

Jobs, Steve Wozniak, and Dan Kottke. Apple I did not get much attention, but the experience of seeing the competition taught Jobs a lot. He left there with a clear idea of what they had to do to make Apple Computer succeed.

Wozniak began work on technical improvements for their next computer, the Apple II. It would have an operating system (designed by Bill Gates and Microsoft) that would load automatically, have color capability, respond faster, and run more quietly because it didn't have a cooling fan. It would also include a keyboard. Meanwhile, Jobs was busy making sure that the way the computer looked would appeal to their customers.

Jobs and Wozniak working together.

He also knew Apple Computer needed a public relations firm to help them market their product. He sought out the best in the business, Regis McKenna. At first, McKenna was not interested in taking on a small, unknown company like Apple Computer as a client. But McKenna had never before met anyone with Steve Jobs's determination. Jobs refused to take no for an answer. Day after day Jobs called McKenna to set up a meeting. Finally, McKenna agreed to meet with him. After they met, Jobs used a tactic that had worked for him before—he refused to leave McKenna's office until McKenna agreed to take them on as a client. Finally, McKenna agreed to represent Apple Computer.

One of the first things McKenna did was have Rob Janoff design a company logo. It was an apple with a bite out of it. The apple would have a color-block design using six colors in order to highlight the fact that the Apple II

Original Apple Computers logo on delivery truck.

was the first color-capable computer to hit the market.

Jobs knew what they needed next: money—and lots of it. They had to pay for McKenna's marketing campaign and the materials they needed to produce the Apple II. He found an investor named Mark Markkula who supplied the money in exchange for a partnership in Apple Computer.

All of their hard work paid off in 1977—Apple II was introduced at the West Coast Computer Faire. The Apple II was a hit with the crowd. When people saw the capabilities of this computer, orders started pouring in.

It was about this same time that Jobs's girlfriend, Chris-Ann Brennan, announced she was pregnant. Jobs was

Jobs with the Apple II.

upset and although he actually was the father of her child, he denied it. He refused to have anything to do with Brennan or the baby. Jobs's reaction was so unexpected that even his friends could not understand his behavior. He had always struggled with the fact that his birth mother had given him up for adoption. He had recently begun searching for her. Brennan was at the All-One Farm when she gave birth to their daughter, Lisa Nicole Brennan-Jobs, on May 17, 1978. Jobs was there when his daughter was born. But for years after her birth, Jobs refused to help Brennan or financially support his child. Eventually, Jobs reunited with his daughter and developed a relationship with her that continued up until his death.

It was also during this period that Jobs found out who

Jobs with daughter, Lisa, in 1989.

his biological parents were. His mother was Joanne Carole Schieble. His father was a Syrian man whose name was Abdulfattah Jandali. He also found out he had a full sister, named Mona Simpson. Even though Jobs and his sister were both adults when they met, they developed a close, loving relationship.

TAKING A BITE OF SUCCESS

Apple Computer grew and grew with great success. By the time Steve Jobs was twenty-four years old, he was a millionaire. The company went public and Apple Computer stock was sold on the stock exchange. Jobs bought a big house, but he kept it simple and uncluttered. It contained almost no furniture—only a Tiffany lamp, a chair, a bed, and a picture of Einstein. Now that Apple Computer was a public company, the decisions were not made by Jobs and Wozniak alone, but by a president and board of directors. By this point, Apple had hundreds of engineers and programmers. After being injured in a plane crash, Wozniak decided to take a leave of absence from Apple and return to college.

But Jobs stayed on at Apple and began work on a new computer he called the Lisa. The project was likely named after his daughter, though some say *Lisa* was an acronym for "Local Integrated Software Architecture." Jobs's ability to think "out of the box" in creative ways had always been one of his strengths. Jobs wanted to add many different innovative features to the Lisa. He pushed the engineers to make the changes, but his stubborn insistence didn't go over very well with others on the design team. They grew more and more frustrated with Jobs until John Sculley, Apple's chief executive officer (CEO) took him off the Lisa project.

After losing command of the Lisa project, Jobs took control of a small project that was under development. It would be called the Macintosh (Mac) named after a MacIntosh apple. The Mac would be very different from the Lisa. By

Mac Lisa computer

the time the Lisa was released, Apple had invested so much time and money into its development that the price of the computer was about $10,000, so it was purchased mostly by businesses. The Mac would be developed and sold keeping the needs of the individual user in mind and would cost about $2,500.

With a small group of talented people working on the Mac, Jobs was at the top of his game. He motivated the Mac team to create something "insanely great." He told them they were like a band of pirates and even hung a pirate flag up to prove it. He insisted they could get the Macintosh ready to ship in less than a year—a seemingly impossible task. He wouldn't take no for an answer. Jobs expected his Mac team of pirates to work long, grueling hours to meet his goal.

Jobs had high expectations about what the designers of the Mac could do. The engineers would show Jobs the software code on which they were working. If the code was not up to Jobs's standards, he would throw it back at them and say it wasn't good enough. His reaction was often harsh, but it did force the design team to produce work that was better than they ever thought possible.

Jobs's abrasive ways meant that many at Apple were not happy with him—including the management. When the Macintosh was released in 1984, it was the first personal computer to use a graphical (symbols and pictures) user interface and a mouse to navigate. But the sales weren't as good as Jobs anticipated they would be. At the time, their rival, IBM, was selling more personal computers than Apple.

ROTTEN APPLE

John Sculley, the one running the company along with the board of directors, fired thirty-year-old Steve Jobs. Suddenly Jobs was banished from the company he had cofounded. Jobs said, "What had been the focus of my entire adult life was gone, and it was devastating."

For a few months, Jobs didn't know what to do. He spent a lot of time alone and traveled around Europe. In time, Jobs came to see that getting fired from Apple was the best thing that could have happened. It freed him to start over—but this time as a very wealthy man. He began a new computer company he named NeXT. About this time, Jobs was speaking at Stanford University, and he spotted a beautiful young woman in the audience who

Jobs with wife, Laurene Powell.

caught his attention. After his presentation, he met her and found out her name was Laurene Powell. They eventually married and had three children together.

In 1985 Jobs's professional life took an unexpected turn when he found out that George Lucas was interested in selling the computer section of his company Lucasfilm. When Lucas worked on the movie *Star Wars*, he found the special effects were difficult to accomplish. He wanted to find a way to do it digitally, so he hired a group of computer graphics experts to work on it. By the time Jobs visited Lucasfilm, he was amazed by what he saw there. The animated graphics they were producing were like nothing else he had ever seen.

After some negotiation with George Lucas, Jobs bought the animation department, and called his new company Pixar. Jobs had never made a movie before, much less an animated movie. But that didn't stop him. He wanted to create movies with high-quality computer graphics. Yet, Jobs understood the story and the characters in a movie must also be compelling.

Jobs brought his creative genius and drive for a quality product to Pixar. He also brought his ability to push his team to do their best work. His friend John Patrick Crecine said, "Steve might be capable of reducing someone to tears, but it's not because he's meanspirited; it's because

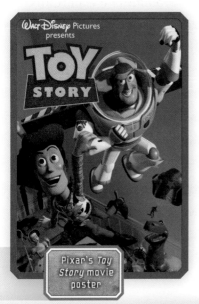

Pixar's *Toy Story* movie poster

he's absolutely single minded, almost manic, in his pursuit of quality and excellence." Jobs led Pixar as they revolutionized the way animated movies are made today. *Toy Story*, the first Pixar-animated full-length feature, was a smash hit. It was the beginning of a long line of blockbuster movies.

While Jobs had been busy establishing his new companies,

NeXT and Pixar, Apple Computer very nearly collapsed. Their competitors were selling more efficient computers for less and the number of Apple computers sold fell dramatically. The leadership at Apple knew they needed to get Jobs back, so they offered to buy NeXT from Jobs for more than $400 million, which brought Jobs back into the Apple family. Then Apple asked Jobs to return as the CEO. At the same time he was running Pixar, Jobs returned to the company he cofounded with Steve Wozniak. He chose to take a salary of only $1 a year—but he was amply compensated with shares of Apple Computer stock, which have continued to increase in value over time. Also during this time, Bill Gates's Microsoft invested $150 million into Apple Computer. Although the two companies were rivals in a few areas, Microsoft produced some software for the Mac.

POLISHING THE APPLE

After he had control of Apple once again, Jobs took the company in a different direction. Jobs had the ability to conceive of the products the public would want, even before they knew they wanted them. It had always been important to him that Apple products work well, but it was also important to him that the design be simple and beautiful. John Sculley, the former CEO of Apple—and the one who

Jobs unveils new iPhone at Apple Worldwide Developers Conference.

had fired Jobs—said, "He's a minimalist and constantly reducing things to their simplest level. It's not simplistic. It's simplified. . . . He simplifies complexity." Jobs used his unique gifts to create Apple's iTunes, iPods, iPhones, and iPads. Each has been a commercial success. More than 10 billion songs have been downloaded from iTunes; more than 304 million iPods, 108 million iPhones, and 25 million iPads have been sold.

In 2004 Jobs was diagnosed with pancreatic cancer. He had surgery and recovered. About a year after his bout with cancer, Jobs gave the commencement speech at Stanford University. Through his remarks that day, he told the audience that the span of each of our lives is limited—so the time each one has should not be wasted. He recalled a quote he once heard that cautioned people to live as if each day was their last. Jobs told the graduates that this statement had stayed with him through the years and had caused him to ask himself, "'If today were the last day of my life, would I want to do what I am about to do today?' And whenever the answer had been 'No' for too many days in a row, I know I need to change something."

But Jobs's health issues weren't over. Four years later, in 2009, Jobs had a liver transplant. Since Jobs felt his health issues were a personal matter, he did not publicly discuss the details of this surgery. Then on January 17, 2011, Jobs sent an email to Apple employees to explain that he would

Jobs attends the grand opening of Apple's flagship store on Fifth Avenue.

take a medical leave of absence to focus on his health, and requested privacy. Jobs also told them he would continue as the chief executive officer of Apple and be involved in major company decisions.

On June 6, 2011, Jobs did what he loved to do—talk about new innovations from Apple. As James Brown's song "I Feel Good" blared, Steve Jobs took the stage at the Apple Worldwide Developers Conference. He was dressed in his usual jeans, black mock turtleneck shirt, and sneakers. Jobs was there to announce Apple's newest product, iCloud.

Jobs unveils iCloud at Apple Worldwide Developers Conference.

He explained how Apple's iCloud would sync your music, photos, documents, and calendar entries to all of your electronic devices including your Mac, iPhone, or iPad. And it would all happen automatically.

Jobs had told the Board of Directors that if the day came that he could no longer do his duty as the CEO of Apple, he would tell them. That day came on August 24, 2011, when Jobs resigned his position and named Tim Cook as his successor.

Steve Jobs had been the creative force behind Apple through the years. He worked to create products that he would like to use himself. He insisted that each one be beautifully designed, be simple to use, and work properly. And he wouldn't take no for an answer.

On October 5, 2011, Steve Jobs died. Many people publicly honored Jobs and his work following his death. One of these tributes came from Bill Gates, who had been Jobs's colleague, competitor, and friend. Gates said, "The world rarely sees someone who has had the profound impact Steve has had, the effects of which will be felt for many generations to come. For those of us lucky enough to get to work with him, it's been an insanely great honor."

Portrait of Steve Jobs, on cover page of apple.com and displayed on an Apple iPad.

JEFF BEZOS

JEFF BEZOS is an entrepreneur who has led the way to buying and selling on the Internet. He is best known for founding Amazon.com.

A NEW FATHER

When Jeffrey Preston Bezos (pronounced Bay-zos) was four, his mother, Jackie Gise, married Mike Bezos, a man who had come to America from Cuba when he was a teenager. Jackie was only seventeen when her son was born in Albuquerque, New Mexico, on January 12, 1964. Her marriage to the boy's father ended after only one year, but Mike Bezos became a loving father to Jeff soon after. When Jeff Bezos was five, his sister, Christina, was born. The next year, his brother, Mark, completed the family.

Bezos was ten years old before he found out the man he called Dad was not his biological father. Jeff Bezos would never know his biological father, and he has always considered Mike Bezos to be his only father.

Jeff Bezos showed signs early on in life that he was mechanically minded. As a toddler the day came when he no longer wanted to sleep in his crib. Young Bezos got a screwdriver and took the crib apart. As Bezos got older, his need to take things apart and put them back together meant that he needed more room. So he took over the family garage as sort of a "science fair central"—the place where he built models out of odd bits and pieces. As his younger siblings got old enough to bother him, they would enter his room without permission. Jeff placed a buzzer on his door that sounded an alarm if they trespassed. Bezos said, "I was constantly booby-trapping the house with various kinds of alarms and some of them were not just audible sounds, but actually like physical booby-traps."

BEZOS MEETS A MAINFRAME

Bezos loved to watch *Star Trek* on television and dreamed that one day he would become an astronaut. He also loved technology of all sorts. In 1974 Bezos got an opportunity few fourth-graders got in those days. Like Bill Gates had had six years before him, Bezos had access to a mainframe computer. (At this point in time, Gates was a student at Harvard and was trying to decide whether or not he should start a business.) The same thing happened at both of their schools. The teachers didn't know what to do with the computer, and they turned it over to the brightest students to figure it out. Bezos and some other kids learned how to program the computer by studying a stack of manuals. When they found out the computer was already programmed to play a *Star Trek* game, they didn't go much further with the programming. But it was his experience with the mainframe that began his love of computers that continues today.

Another thing Bezos loved was the summers he spent

with his grandparents Mattie and Lawrence Preston Gise. At the time of these summer visits, his grandfather ran a twenty-five-thousand-acre ranch in Cotulla, Texas. Each summer, Bezos helped his grandfather repair everything from windmills to huge machinery.

Bezos also spent time traveling around the country with his grandparents. They were part of a group of people who caravanned in their Airstream recreational vehicle (RV) along with hundreds of other members of the Caravan Club. Bezos had always been great at math. So as he traveled along, he spent a lot of time working out statistical problems like the gas mileage for their vehicle.

The summer he was ten years old, Bezos and his grandparents were on one of their road trips. His grandmother smoked—a lot. He had heard a statistic somewhere that suggested that every puff of a cigarette took time off of the smoker's life. Bezos crunched the numbers. Then he stuck his head through the haze of secondhand smoke into the front seat to share his latest calculation. He expected to be complimented on his math skills as he announced to his grandmother, "At two minutes per puff, you've taken nine years off your life!"

He didn't get the reaction he anticipated. His grandmother cried.

His grandfather pulled their vehicle off of the road. He got out of the car and walked around to open the car door. As he got out of the car, Bezos didn't know what to expect. Would he be punished? Finally, his grandfather said, "Jeff, one day you'll understand that it's harder to be kind than clever." Bezos never forgot that day.

As Bezos grew up, he loved to read and he loved school. He worked hard on his studies and considered himself to be sort of a nerd. He rarely got into trouble, but did get his library privileges taken away one day at school for laughing too loudly. All through his life, Bezos has had a joyous, distinctive laugh that was once described as "a streak of exclamation points." By the time he was in high school, the Bezos family had moved to Miami, Florida. He grew more

Apple II computer

and more interested in computers. When he was in the eleventh grade, Bezos owned one of Steve Jobs's computers—the Apple II Plus. He was the valedictorian and the class president by the time he graduated from Palmetto High School.

CHANGING COURSE

After high school, Bezos chose to attend Princeton

University, where he planned to pursue a degree in physics. But once he took some classes in the field, he realized other students were much more suited for studying physics than he was. So he changed his mind and started working toward a degree in computer

Princeton University
(Library)

science. Since Bezos had always had an interest in space exploration, he became the president of Students for the Exploration and Development of Space (SEDS). Bezos hoped someday he might get the chance to go into space himself.

Bezos graduated *summa cum laude* (with highest honors) from Princeton in 1986 with degrees in electrical engineering and computer science. He got a job at Fitel, a Wall Street firm, where he worked studying trends. His job was sort of a mixture of computers and finance. In 1988 he left Fitel to go to work at Bankers Trust Company. Bezos became a vice president there and led the development of computer systems that helped manage more than $250 billion in assets. Next, he went to D.E. Shaw & Co., an

Bezos with wife,
MacKenzie Tuttle.

investment organization, where he became senior vice president. It was while he worked at Shaw that he met and fell in love with MacKenzie Tuttle, also a Princeton graduate. They married in 1992.

SEIZE THE DAY

By this time, about seventeen years had passed since Bill Gates and Microsoft had set the goal of putting a personal computer in every home and office. The Internet was just beginning to be widely used by computer users. (The original Internet was called ARPANET—Advanced Research Projects Agency Network—and had been developed and used by the defense department. The government eventually allowed the public to access what is now known as the Internet.) Bezos was fascinated by the Internet. As he was working in his office in a high-rise building in Manhattan one day in May 1994, he saw an incredible statistic. The Internet usage was growing at a rate of 2,300 percent a year.

For thirty-year-old Bezos it was a wake-up call. He wondered about what business opportunities this might create. He began to think about different sorts of products that could be sold on the Internet. He did some research on successful mail-order companies. Bezos considered if it would be possible to sell books on the Internet. It seemed like a good idea. There were too many books in print to list them in any sort of paper catalog. But on the Internet there was a limitless amount of space, giving you the possibility to be able to sell any book that had ever been printed.

Bezos wanted to learn more about the book industry. As it happened, the American Booksellers Association (ABA) convention was in Los Angeles, so he flew to California. He walked around and talked to publishers. He was delighted to find out that book wholesalers already had databases of their books that were organized and could be listed online easily.

He thought his idea of selling books on the Internet would work. When he returned home to New York, Bezos took the idea to his boss, D. E. Shaw. But Shaw had no interest in pursuing the idea.

Bezos considered leaving his job to give it a try. But then again, should he leave a great job over an idea that might not work? He discussed it with his wife who told him she would support his decision either way. Bezos told his boss he was quitting. Shaw cautioned him to wait and think about it for another forty-eight hours before he made a final decision. Bezos thought it over carefully, and knew he had to try. He said, "It was like the wild, wild West, a new frontier. And I knew that if I didn't try this, I would regret it. And that would be inescapable."

Bezos needed people to invest money into his company before he could begin. Some people told him his idea would never work. When he called his parents to tell them his plan to sell books online, his father had never even heard of the Internet. Even though Jackie and Mike Bezos didn't really understand what their son planned to do, they loved and trusted him enough to invest $300,000 of their money into his dream. Bezos knew that most start-up companies like his failed, so he warned his parents and other investors that there was a 70 percent chance they would lose their money, and cautioned them not to invest it unless they could afford to lose it.

He and his wife made the decision to leave New York and move to the Seattle, Washington. If they were located in the Northwest, they could be close to Ingram, a major book warehouse. Another factor was that they would have access to the many skilled computer programmers who lived in the area.

FLOATING DOWN THE AMAZON

On July 4, 1994, Jeff and MacKenzie Bezos flew to his parents' home. They went there first in order to pick up a 1988 Chevy Blazer his father gave them. MacKenzie drove toward Seattle while her husband worked on writing a business plan. He thought about calling the company Abracadabra, but the word seemed too long. When he talked to his lawyer on the phone, Bezos told him he was going to shorten the company name to Cadabra. His lawyer misunderstood him and thought he said *cadaver*. If his own lawyer didn't understand the name the first time he heard it, Bezos knew it wasn't the right choice. Bezos decided to change the name to Amazon, to honor one of the longest rivers in the world.

In Bellevue, Washington, Jeff and MacKenzie Bezos rented a two-bedroom house and planned to work out of the garage. Bezos bought some doors from Home Depot for less than $60 each to use as desks, and ran extension cords from the house for power. The first person he hired was Shel Kaphan, a gifted computer programmer who set up a system that would be easy to use. By June 1995, the website was ready for a test run. Three hundred people tested the website and it worked perfectly.

On July 16, 1995, Amazon.com opened for business on

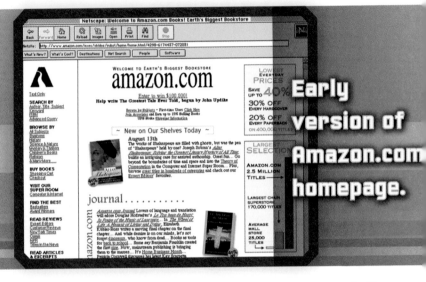

Early version of Amazon.com homepage.

the Internet. In anticipation they had rigged up a bell to ring each time they received a book order. When the first order came in on the first day, the bell rang out. Then as orders started coming in faster, the bell rang over and over again. After the first few days, they had to disconnect the bell—it was ringing too often. Bezos knew within the first few days that Amazon was going to grow to be bigger than he first thought.

Within thirty days, Amazon.com had received book orders from all fifty states and forty-five foreign countries. By September they had sales of $20,000 a week. Bezos hired more people. During the day they worked at their company tasks. Then at night, everyone worked together to ship books that had been ordered. Amazon quickly outgrew the garage.

Amazon.com was so successful that it went public in 1997. The value of stock went up, and since Bezos had lots of shares of stock—he was suddenly a millionaire. Jeff and MacKenzie Bezos built a

Bezos holding a copy of *Fluid Concepts and Creative Analogies*—the first book ever sold on Amazon.

big home on Lake Washington, near the home of Bill Gates.

Bezos constantly looked for ways to improve the Amazon.com site and their customers' satisfaction. He introduced some improvements to the site like customer feedback, the one-click purchase button, purchase suggestions, order verification, and credit card encryption for safer transactions. They built warehouses in Delaware to ship orders faster to the East Coast, and one in Nevada to ship orders faster to the West Coast.

Next Bezos set his sights to sell more than just books, announcing that Amazon would sell anything that a customer might want to buy online. He had built the "Earth's

Bookshelves inside Amazon's warehouse.

biggest bookstore" and he planned to turn it into the "Earth's biggest anything store." He succeeded with that, too.

AN EMPTY BOOK BAG

In 2001 Bezos turned his attention back to books—but in a very different way. He said, "I've actually asked myself, 'Why do I love these physical objects? Why do I love the smell of glue and ink?' The answer is that I associate that smell with all those worlds I have been transported to. What we love is the words and ideas." He developed a device that would change how books could be read in the future. He introduced an electronic reading device he called the Kindle. He chose the name because he thought it evoked the feeling of the ignition of knowledge.

Explaining how the Kindle would work, Bezos said, "The vision is that you should be able to get any book—not just any book in print, but any book that's ever been in print—on this device in less than a minute." Apple Computer's Steve Jobs predicted the Kindle would fail because he thought that people didn't read much anymore. (In 2010 Jobs introduced the Apple iPad, which can be used as an e-reader.)

The Kindle was a success. As the years went by, consumers grew more and more accustomed to e-readers. By mid-2010 Amazon had sold 2.38 billion e-books—more e-book copies than hardcover copies of books. Bezos believes books will go away eventually. He said, "the physical book really has had a 500-year run. It's probably the most successful technology ever. . . . But no technology, not even one as elegant as the book, lasts forever."

Bezos with Kindle DX.

INFINITY AND BEYOND

Bezos and his wife have four children. His success with Amazon.com has made him a billionaire many times over. Yet he has never forgotten his love of space. Now he can seriously pursue his passion for the final frontier. He founded a company named Blue Origin, which has space tourism as its goal. The company logo is two turtles standing on the earth reaching for the stars. Underneath are the Latin words *gradatim ferociter*, the company motto that means "step by step, ferociously."

He plans to reach the goal of space tourism, but he wants to move slowly to ensure safety. Bezos hired a small team of gifted people who have a passion for space and built a huge research and development facility in Kent, Washington— about twenty minutes south of Seattle. He also bought

Bezos's land in Culberson County, Texas.

165,000 acres in west Texas, in Culberson County, to use for a launch complex.

For the first few years as their work began, little was known about Blue Origin. As they made some information available to the public, they announced their project's name would be New Shepard. The name pays homage to NASA astronaut Alan

Alan Shepard on the moon.

Shepard, the first American to fly a suborbital mission, which took place on May 5, 1961. (Shepard later walked and hit golf balls on the moon.) When it is completed, Blue Origin's *New Shepard* will be a rocket-propelled craft that can fly people into suborbital space—for a price.

The team is working to develop systems that will ultimately be used in *New Shepard*. The first test craft, *Goddard*, was ready to launch on November 13, 2006. Friends and family of the Blue Origin staff gathered to watch. *Goddard* looked like a giant gumdrop with legs that went straight up and staight down during its successful flight. Blue Origin plans to build and launch additional test vehicles during this research and development phase.

In the last few years, NASA began working with independent companies to promote space exploration. In 2009 it was announced that five companies would receive funds from NASA. Blue Origin received $3.7 million to assist their development of space transportation systems that could be used in the future. In 2011, NASA announced that Blue Origin would receive another $22 million.

Work at Blue Origin continues. On May 6, 2011, another test flight was successful. But on August 24, 2011, an unmanned test flight crashed. Although it was a set-back for Blue Origin, they are already working on the next development vehicle. When the project is finished, *New Shepard* will have a crew capsule (CC) where the astronauts and paying customers and equipment will ride. It will also have a propulsion module (PM). From the west Texas launch site, *New Shepard* will take off straight up, accelerate for about two and a half minutes, then shut off the rocket engines and coast into space. It will reach the suborbital level where travelers can see Earth's atmosphere and experience zero gravity for a few brief moments. After the CC and PM separate, each piece will land back on Earth separately—to be used again.

New Shepard will take people to the edge of space and

safely bring them down again. Jeff Bezos can't wait to take the trip himself. Even though his thoughts are often filled with his boyhood dream of space travel, Bezos has his feet firmly planted on the ground. On May 30, 2010, he was the commencement speaker at Princeton University. Bezos shared with them the story of the day when he was ten, when his smoking statistic made his grandmother cry. He told them about the lesson his grandfather taught him that day. Speaking to some of the world's brightest young minds, Bezos reminded the graduates that "Cleverness is a gift, kindness is a choice."

Jeff Bezos saw the Internet as an opportunity that would allow him to do what had never been done before. He envisioned a bookstore that was not bound by shelf space. Bezos looked for a way to sell books online, and succeeded. Then he looked for a way to sell anything online, and succeeded. Now he is looking for a way to take people into space— and with his track record, success can't be far away.

Bezos is named *Time* magazine's Person of the Year in 1999.

SERGEY BRIN

SERGEY BRIN is a computer scientist and businessman. He is best known for being one of the cofounders of Google.

MOTHER RUSSIA

In the 1970s many people in the Soviet Union held prejudices regarding Jewish people. This made it difficult, but not impossible, for Jewish people to get a higher education. Michael and Eugenia Brin were fortunate—they both were able to receive university degrees. Originally, Michael Brin wanted to study astronomy, but the government excluded Jews from the field. He changed to the study of mathematics and graduated with honors and went on to earn a doctorate degree.

Their son, Sergey Mikhailovich Brin, was born on August 21, 1973, in Moscow, Russia. At the time, they lived in a 350-square-foot apartment, along with Michael Brin's mother. During the summer of 1977, Michael Brin attended a mathematical conference in Poland. He was exposed to people from the United States for the first time and had the chance to hear about life in the West. He came home and announced to his wife and mother that they could no longer stay in their own country—that they must leave. But Eugenia Brin wasn't sure they should leave. After all, they had good jobs, and they had their young son to consider. In the end, it was concern for their child that made her decide to go. The Brins didn't want their son to face the same sort of discrimination they had faced. They decided to leave Russia not only for their own future but for their son's future.

Because of strict governmental control, the Brins understood it could be dangerous for them to apply for a visa to
leave the country. But they were determined to try. As soon
as the family applied for the exit visa in September 1978,
Michael Brin was fired from his job. For money, he began
translating technical books into English. Eugenia Brin told
her coworkers she was leaving her position because she
got a different job. In May 1979 their visas were approved.
They were fortunate to get out when they did because soon
after, very few Russians were allowed to leave the country.

DISCOVERING AMERICA

The Brin family arrived in America on October 25.
Michael Brin got a job teaching math at the University of
Maryland. Eugenia Brin worked first at a consulting firm,
then as a research scientist at the NASA Goddard Space
Flight Center. Even though they had very little money, the
Brins decided to enroll their son in a private school, the
Paint Branch Montessori School. A Montessori education
promotes a method of learning that allows each child to
learn at his or her own individual pace by choosing from
a variety of appropriate learning activities. When six-
year-old Sergey Brin began school, he didn't know much
English and had a thick Russian accent. That first year
was difficult for him, but then he made the adjustment to

his new country and language. He always had a mischie-
vous twinkle in his eyes and his father joked, "Sergey was
a good boy, when he was asleep."

Brin got his first computer, a Commodore 64, when he
was nine years old. He had always been good with numbers,
but by the time he was in middle school, it was clear he was
a math prodigy. His school brought in a special teacher for
him and a few other advanced students. Education was a
priority in the Brin family—not only for Sergey, but also for
his younger brother, Sam, who was born in 1987.

During the summer of 1990, Brin's father took his
family, along with a group of high school math students,
to the Soviet Union for an exchange program. It was a
chance for the Brins to see the family they left behind and
their home country once again. Sergey Brin saw for himself the bleak situation
as the Soviet Union
was falling apart. He
understood as never
before the life he had
been spared because
his parents left their
home. He thanked his
father for moving them
out of Russia.

The Commodore 64

WHIZ KID

Brin attended Eleanor Roosevelt High School in Greenbelt, Maryland. When he graduated high school in three years, he had already earned one year's worth of college credits. He went to college at the University of Maryland at College Park. During the summers, he worked programming algorithms (step-by-step mathematical procedures to solve problems) for places such as the University of Maryland Institute for Advanced Computer Studies, and the University of Maryland Systems Designs and Analysis Group. In 1993 he graduated at the age of nineteen with honors and a bachelor's degree in mathematics and computer science.

Brin decided to go to graduate school at Stanford, located in Palo Alto, California. Since he would be on his own at school, before leaving for the West Coast, he decided

University of Maryland at College Park

he should learn to cook. Along the way he learned to prepare a dish he called Chernobyl Chili, which he cooked in the microwave for forty-five minutes.

Brin realized the individual attention he'd gotten at the University of Maryland had equipped him well for Stanford.

He felt he was better prepared than his classmates who came from MIT and Harvard. Brin had a quick wit and an air of self-confidence about him. At Stanford he would walk into his professors' offices without knocking. One of his advisers said of him, "He was a brash young man. But he was so smart, it just oozed out of him."

Brin took advantage of the beautiful California weather and took classes in sailing, swimming, and scuba diving. When his father asked him if he was taking any advanced courses, in his usual clever manner he answered that he was taking advanced swimming. Brin also loved gymnastics and even tried the flying trapeze at circus school in nearby San Francisco. He preferred to work on difficult mathematical projects more than take regular classes, and he published dozens of technical papers.

In 1995 Brin published the first of many technical papers and he was almost finished with his studies for a master's degree. That spring he was one of the grad students who gave tours of the campus and nearby San Francisco to students who were considering attending Stanford.

It was on one of these tours that Sergey Brin met Larry Page for the first time. Neither one liked the other. Neither one could have imagined that they would one day be best friends. Neither one could have imagined that—together—they would change the way the world finds information.

LARRY PAGE

LARRY PAGE is a computer scientist and businessman. He is best known for being one of the cofounders of Google.

A COMPUTER FAMILY

Lawrence (Larry) Edward Page was born into a computer-loving family on March 26, 1973. His father, Carl Page, was one of the first people to enter the new field of computer science and earn a Ph.D. Larry's mother, Gloria Page, had a master's degree in computer science and worked as a database consultant. Even his brother, Carl Jr., who is nine years older than Larry, was into computers. (Years later, his brother sold his company eGroups.com to Yahoo! for $432 million.)

Because of the Pages' work, the family had all sorts of electronics. Even as a young boy, Larry Page was free to play with the equipment in their home in East Lansing, Michigan. He loved everything about electronic gadgets and he knew he wanted to invent things. When Carl Jr. came home from college, he brought his little brother leftover electronic devices from his computer lab classes. Young Page learned about electronics by tinkering with the parts.

He got his first computer in 1978. It was an Exidy Sorcerer, a popular brand in Europe. It was huge and expensive. To make it work, Carl Jr. had to write the operating system. One of the first things six-year-old Larry Page did on the computer was type the words from the book *Frog and Toad Together* into a word processing

Exidy Sorcerer computer

program. In elementary school Page did his homework assignments on the computer and handed in printed copies to his teachers.

As he grew up, Page sometimes played the saxophone and considered Nikola Tesla (who invented the alternating electric current) his hero. He especially loved to read computer magazines like *Popular Science*. He wanted to know how things worked—not only how the electronics worked but the mechanical parts, too. He was interested in technology, but he was also interested in social issues like politics. During middle school, Page's Cub Scout leader remembered him as "an independent thinker." By the time he was twelve, Page knew he would someday start a company.

FOLLOWING FOOTSTEPS

After he graduated from high school, Page attended the University of Michigan, Ann Arbor, like his parents and brother had before him. While he was in college, he decided to create a printer that would produce

University of Michigan

big images, so he built the electronic and mechanical parts to drive it and built the printer out of legos. Page also spent a lot of time thinking about transportation issues and sustainable energy. He even tried to convince the University of Michigan that it should build a monorail to stretch the two miles between central and north campus. But they wouldn't do it.

One summer during college he attended a summer institute called LeaderShape. This program, which still exists, was designed to encourage its participants to become powerful leaders by motivating them to create powerful visions, build successful teams, and implement action plans. The lessons Page learned at LeaderShape would stay with him forever.

In 1995 Page graduated with a bachelor's degree in engineering from the University of Michigan. To get a master's degree, twenty-two-year-old Larry Page considered Stanford University. He traveled to Palo Alto, California, to take a tour of the Stanford campus.

It was there that he met Sergey Brin for the first time.

THE MEETING

On a spring day in 1995, Page was assigned to a group led by Brin, who was to show them the campus and city sights. For about two days, they walked around together—and they disagreed about everything.

Page thought Brin was obnoxious and argumentative.

Brin thought Page was obnoxious and argumentative.

In spite of his tour guide, Page ultimately decided to attend Stanford. He was a long way from Michigan, and would later recall, "At first, it was pretty scary. I kept complaining to my friends that I was going to get sent home on the bus. It didn't quite happen that way, however."

Page and Brin had gotten off to a rocky start in the spring, but each of them enjoyed the intellectual challenge of the other. Each time they talked they got to know each other better, and they found they had a lot in common. They had similar interests in research. They both liked to have intellectual debates that would challenge their opponent's views. They had both attended Montessori schools. Each of their families valued education and independent learning. And although Brin was Jewish and Page's mother was Jewish, neither of their families was religious.

By the fall of 1995, they were good friends who spent a lot of time together—so much time that around Stanford they were known as LarryandSergey. They even started working together on a project. Since they shared similar interests in the Internet—Page studied the links to pages on the Web, while Brin studied data mining (finding information

William Gates Computer Science Building at Stanford University

from different sources and analyzing it for practical uses). Along with other grad students, they worked in the brand-new William Gates Computer Science building, built with money donated by Microsoft's Bill Gates. They settled into their work in their third-floor office and put in many long hours.

Only a few months after Page got to Stanford, his father had trouble breathing and went to the hospital. Carl Page had had polio when he was young, and his medical history complicated his condition. He died two months later, leaving his son completely devastated. Even though he was saddened by the loss, Page continued his work.

THE SEARCH BEGINS

At this point in time, when a person typed a keyword into a search engine, thousands of web pages turned up. Some web pages were relevant but many only contained a random mention of the word. The search results were in no sort of order at all. When a user was looking for specific information, these searches were not very helpful.

Page started looking at the links that were found on web pages. He thought links were in some ways similar to citations a writer used in a research paper. He wanted to study web links in a systematic way.

Page (top) and Brin (bottom)

Then twenty-three-year-old Page had a dream—a vivid dream. He woke up thinking about his dream and grabbed a pen and pad to make notes on his thoughts. "When I suddenly woke up, I was thinking: What if we could download the whole Web, and just keep the links . . . and I grabbed a pen and started writing." The more he thought about the idea, the more he liked it. He went to talk to his adviser, Terry Winograd, about it. Page told him he thought he could download the entire Web in a couple of weeks. Although Winograd knew it would take much longer than that, he said nothing and just nodded at Page.

In March 1996 Page began searching web links using a "spider," which is a program that automatically searches through Internet web pages (called web crawling). Page started his spider on his own home page at Stanford. The web pages gathered by the spider were then indexed. As Page studied the results, he realized the number of links to a web page was a factor in determining the relevance of a search word. He also realized that some links to a web page were more important than others. (For example, a link to a NASA website from the U.S. government would be more valuable than a link to NASA from a teenager who logs on to look at cool images from space.)

Brin had been considering ideas for his thesis project, and he decided to join Page. He said, "I talked to lots of research groups and this was the most exciting project, both because it tackled the web, which represents human knowledge, and because I liked Larry."

GENTLEMEN, START YOUR ENGINES

The goal of the project was to create a better search engine than those already in use on the Internet. They needed an algorithm that would allow them to rank the importance of web pages, which Brin provided. Brin and Page developed

PageRank, naming it after Page. The method used to figure out the rank of each site is complex. It used many different techniques to determine the importance of each web page, including things like the font size, how close together the words are, what other documents say about the page, and how good the links are.

With PageRank, they could order websites according to their relevancy to the keyword. The results were amazing. When PageRank was used, the most relevant or important websites were at the top of the list and the least relevant or important were at the bottom. As they worked on the project, Brin and Page realized the results they got from PageRank were better than the results they could get from AltaVista or Excite, the popular search engines in use at the time.

Page and Brin made changes and improvements to the web ranking program and renamed it BackRub. Their program worked by creating a massive index of all the websites they could find—and this massive index took up lots of space on computer hard drives. Since the number of websites available on the Internet grew every day, they needed more and more computers in order to contain the fast-growing index. They got computers from everywhere and anywhere. Page's dorm room was turned into a huge

computer complex. Brin's room became the office and programming center. By 1996, they had turned BackRub into
a search engine. As soon as it was available, the students,
faculty, and the administration at Stanford began using it.
The news about this efficient search engine quickly spread
by word of mouth. Soon the massive system used nearly
half of all of Stanford's Internet network capabilities—and
they would occasionally crash the system. Fortunately,
the Stanford administration didn't hassle them about the
resources they used.

ANY OTHER NAME

By 1997, Page and Brin decided they needed to rename BackRub, and considered lots of possibilities. They finally settled on Google. The name comes from the mathematical term *googol*, for a one followed by one hundred zeros. It seemed to them a good match to represent the limitless amount of information on the Internet.

Brin designed the Google home page. Most search engine home pages were busy-looking with lots of text and links. Brin's design was the exact opposite. The Google home page would be simple and uncluttered. It had a white background and used basic colors. Early on, Brin knew Google was something special, saying, "I am sometimes something of a lazy person, so when I end up spending a lot of time using something myself—as I did with Google in the earliest of days, I knew it was a big deal."

ENDLESS GROWTH

Their need for more and more computers continued to grow. Page and Brin borrowed computers from anyone who would lend them—and if an owner never asked for one back, they kept it. They didn't have much money, so they bought parts and built their own machines. They maxed out three credit cards buying hard disks. They made cases out of Legos to hold all their hard drives.

In March 1998 Page and Brin had a meeting with an AltaVista representative, and offered to sell their superior search engine, Google, to them. AltaVista did not want to buy it. Neither did Excite or Yahoo!. They did get some valuable advice from one of these meetings. Yahoo!'s cofounder David Filo told the guys they should take a leave of absence from their Ph.D. studies at Stanford and start their own search engine company.

At first they didn't know what to do. Neither one was comfortable with the idea of leaving their doctoral studies. When Brin's parents found out he was taking a leave from his doctoral program they were upset. The deciding factor

Yahoo! cofounders Jerry Yang and David Filo

was that Stanford University told them that if they tried to start a company and it failed, they could return to the Ph.D. program.

Now that they had decided to go into business, they needed a lot of money and started looking for some investors. In August 1998 they met with Andy Bechtolsheim, cofounder of Sun Microsystems, one of the greats of Silicon Valley. Page and Brin explained their search engine to him. Bechtolsheim liked what he heard and said, "This is the single best idea I have heard in years. I want to be part of this." Bechtolsheim took out his checkbook and wrote a check to Google Inc. for $100,000. Page and Brin celebrated by eating at Burger King.

GOOGLE IS BORN

But Google Inc. didn't exist officially, so the two held on to the check for a few weeks while they went through the process of incorporating their new company. On September 7, 1998, Google Inc. officially came into existence with Page as its CEO. They sought out additional investors in their family and friends and ultimately raised $1 million to start their company. One of their investors was Jeff Bezos of Amazon.com, who put in $250,000.

The next step was to move their computers and equipment

out of Stanford to a place of their own. Susan Wojcicki, a friend of Brin's, had a house in Menlo Park, California, and needed help making her house payment. She rented out the garage of her house to them for $1,700 a month. She first thought the guys would be there while she was at work, but as it turned out they were there 24/7, working, raiding the refrigerator, and sitting in the hot tub.

Even during the testing phase Google was handling about one hundred thousand queries a day. Google was gaining in popularity as more and more people used the site. They had to hire eight people to handle the workload. By early 1999, Google outgrew Wojcicki's garage, so they moved into some offices in Palo Alto. Everything was going well. From the

Wojcicki's house in Menlo Park, California.

beginning, their mission was to organize information and make it both accessible and useful to users.

ONE OF A KIND

Early on, Page and Brin determined that they didn't want Google to be a conventional company—they wanted to be unique. Every Friday they held a TGIF celebration where all the employees got together, and Page and Brin would inform them about everything that had happened that week. Other search engine companies wanted to keep users on their sites as long as possible, but Google was just the opposite. Google wanted their users to come to their site, get the desired information, and move away from their site as soon as possible. They decided on a list of ten things they always wanted to keep in mind:

1. Focus on the user: They determined their first concern would be the user—they made sure the home page was easy to use and loaded web pages instantly.

2. Do one thing really well: They focused their attention on creating an accurate search engine.

3. Fast is better: They determined they would deliver the answers to users' questions in the shortest time possible.

4. Democracy on the Web: They would use ranking methods based on links for millions of users to evaluate the

importance of a web page.

5. You don't have to be at your desk to get your questions answered: They wanted users to have access to their search engine from mobile phones and other portable devices.

6. You can make money without doing evil: They would make money by offering their search capabilities to other companies and by selling advertising. They also committed that they would not accept pop-up ads that covered the results and that the advertising would be relevant to users' searches and clearly marked as advertising.

7. More information is out there: They committed themselves to continually look for ways to gain access to more and more of the world's information.

8. Global access to information: They wanted to make information available all over the world and in every language.

9. Serious without a suit: They wanted the Google workplace to be casual—a place where bright, creative people would work hard and have fun.

10. Being great isn't enough: They determined to set high, sometimes unattainable goals, in order to stretch themselves to find innovative ways to make Google better.

MAKING MONEY

Page and Brin had figured out how to make a successful search engine. But they were not making any money. Page said, "We always kind of figured that if we did a good job of providing the right information for everybody in the world, all the time, that would be an important thing to do." But eventually a company must make money to stay in business.

Ultimately, they figured out how to make money on Google through advertising. Because Google was a search engine with keywords typed in by the user, they were able to match product advertisements to those keywords. The advertising would be linked to the user's interest. For example, a user who searched for "baseball" might be interested in sports-related products, so he or she might see ads for sports clothing or sports drinks. These innovative ideas came from Google's first (and current) marketing manager, Susan Wojcicki, the woman in whose garage Google began. Wojcicki is now a senior vice president who oversees advertising on Google. Another way they made a profit was that companies like Yahoo! (which had previously rejected the offer to buy Google) hired them to become their default search engine.

Page and Brin were in their twenties and running the

Schmidt (center) with Brin (left) and Page (right).

entire company. By June 1999, Sequoia Capital and Kleiner Perkins had invested $25 million into Google. In August Page and Brin moved their offices to Mountain View, California. Their investors thought it would benefit them if they had an experienced executive to help them, in a way to give them some adult supervision. In order to get a better idea of what it took to run a successful tech company, they met with several successful men, including Steve Jobs and Jeff Bezos. Page and Brin wanted Steve Jobs to be the CEO of Google, but by that time Jobs was happy to be back at Apple. On August 6, 2001, Dr. Eric Schmidt took over as the Google CEO. Schmidt came to Google with lots of experience both in the world of technology and in business. He had been on the research staff at the Computer Science Lab of Xerox Palo Alto Research Center (PARC), and had been in management at two different computer companies—CEO of Novell and chief technology officer at Sun Microsystems. With Schmidt as Google's CEO, Larry Page became the president of products, and Sergey Brin became the president of technology.

Schmidt, Page, and Brin worked closely together as the number of users and employees grew and grew. By the end of 2000, they had indexed 1.3 billion web pages, which if printed out would have been about seventy miles high. And they anticipated the amount would double each year. Even as their business was growing, both Page and Brin maintained their motto of "Don't be evil" and had the desire to do the best they could for their users.

THE GOOGLEPLEX

In March of 2004 they moved into their new offices in Mountain View called the Googleplex. Later that year, in August, Google became a public company. Since they wanted their complex to have a campus atmosphere, they share offices. Page and Brin still share an office together,

Google headquarters in Mountain View, California.

with several flat-screen computer monitors lining the walls.

In the Googleplex, the atmosphere is relaxed. Google doesn't care what their employees wear, as long as they wear something. Google provides their employees with lots of perks, including three free meals a day served in several different cafés, massages, yoga class, and the freedom to play pool, play volleyball, swim in the lap pool, or play roller hockey. Today TGIF meetings are done by videoconference, which go out to remote locations and are recorded so that employees in other time zones can watch later.

Part of their casual attitude can be seen in the Google

doodle. This is the name given to the Google logo when it celebrates a person, holiday, or event. The doodles do not change every day, but in the United States more than three hundred doodles have appeared through the years. The doodles have become an important part of the Google home page. An archive of Google doodles can be seen at www.google.com/logos.

Every Google employee is supposed to work on the 70-20-10 principle. 70 percent of their time is to go to the primary work of search and advertising, 20 percent to related ideas connected to the main work, and 10 percent to work on new, outside-the-box ideas. Page and Brin believe the best ideas are born out of the 10 percent outside-the-box time—like Paul Buchheit's development of Gmail.

In 2004 Page and Brin were selected by Barbara Walters as two of the ten most fascinating people of the year. During the interview she asked them if having parents who

Selection of Google doodles

were college professors was a major factor behind their success. Instead of this being the most important thing, they both credited their education in Montessori schools, which trained them to be self-motivated and gave them the freedom to do things their own way.

THE NEXT PROJECT

It seems the creative ideas coming from Google never end. They keep about one hundred new projects under development at one time—most of them are kept secret. Page says they usually try ten things that don't work before they find one thing that does work. Through the years,

Brin with wife, Anne Wojcicki.

they have developed many innovative products, including Google Toolbar, Google News, Google News Archive, Google Scholar, Google Maps, Google Earth, Google Street View, Google Docs, Google Translate, Art Project, and Picasa.

By 2007 both Google guys were ready to settle down. In May, Sergey Brin married

Anne Wojcicki on a private island in the Bahamas. Anne is Susan Wojcicki's sister and owner of her own biotech company that provides genetic information to individuals. The bride and groom swam to a sandbar, where they exchanged vows while wearing swimsuits.

In December 2007 Larry Page married Lucy Southworth on a private island in the Caribbean. Lucy was a doctoral student at Stanford working on a biomedical informatics degree. Two years later, both Page and Brin became fathers—each having a son.

The Google guys got a perk in 2007 that none of the other Silicon Valley titans had ever had: a prime parking spot for their company jets. Only a few miles from their

Moffett Field, where Page and Brin park their Google jet.

headquarters in Mountain View, California, is Moffett Field, an airport run by NASA. It is not usually open to private aircraft. In exchange for $1.3 million a year, Page and Brin have permission to park their customized wide-body Boeing 767-200 jet, as well as their other jets at the Field. This agreement not only makes it convenient for the Google executives to travel, but the money helps defray NASA's costs. Another perk for NASA is that they have permission to put instruments and researchers on some Google jet flights to gather scientific information like studying meteor showers. In 2008 a German-built fighter jet was added to the fleet.

BOYS TO MEN

By the end of 2010, the time had come to make some changes in the executive structure of Google—the Google boys no longer needed adult supervision. Page, Brin, and Schmidt worked out the details of the change together. Page would become the CEO. Brin would work on new products. Schmidt would have an advisory role as the executive chairman.

Today Google gets hundreds of millions of queries each day from users all over the world. It is one of the largest computer systems in the world with hundreds of thousands of servers that store indexed websites. Google is available in 130 languages, including Klingon (the fictional language from Star Trek). They have 20,000 employees and offices in cities all over the world. In 2010 Google reported they brought in 29.3 billion dollars. After expenses, they made a profit of 8.5 billion dollars.

In their late thirties, Page and Brin have set their sights and their profits on using technology in a variety of areas. They are working on projects that include artificial intelligence and a car that can drive itself. They also want to reduce automotive carbon emissions and make cars safer. On the East Coast, they have invested in wind farms to produce electricity.

Brin and Page

Brin and Page

Somehow, Page and Brin have kept sight of what is most important. In 2009 Larry Page was the commencement speaker at the University of Michigan, from which he, his parents, and his brother graduated. He wore his father's academic hood and held his father's diploma. He recalled a trip he and his wife took to India. In spite of the work the Bill & Melinda Gates Foundation is doing to eradicate polio, polio still exists there. In India Page and his wife saw a young boy with a limp leg from polio. Page was moved by the sight because his father had died from complications of polio. Page, one of the world's wealthiest men, reminded the graduates, "Just like me, your families brought you here, and you brought them here. Please keep them close and remember: they are what really matters in life."

Page and Brin were asked how it felt to have great wealth. Page said, "If we were motivated by money, we would have sold the company a long time ago and ended up on a beach."

Brin said, "From my parents, I certainly learned to be frugal and to be happy without very many things. It's interesting—I still find myself not wanting to leave anything on the plate uneaten. I still look at prices. I try to force myself to do this less, not to be so frugal. But I was raised being happy with not so much."

Page and Brin's friendship is as strong as ever and each of them feels fortunate to have the other. Together they have made Google a huge success. In some ways, success hasn't changed them at all. They still wear T-shirts, jeans, and sneakers to work and still sometimes celebrate milestones by going to Burger King.

MARK ZUCKERBERG

MARK ZUCKERBERG is a computer programmer and businessman. He is best known for creating Facebook.

QUESTIONS, QUESTIONS, QUESTIONS

Mark Elliot Zuckerberg asked a lot of questions when he was a child. His father said, "For Mark, if he asked for something, *yes* by itself would work, but *no* required much more. If you were going to say no to him, you had better be prepared with a strong argument backed by facts, experiences, logic, reasons. We envisioned him becoming a lawyer one day, with a near 100% success rate of convincing juries."

But being a lawyer would not be part of Zuckerberg's future.

Mark Zuckerberg was born on May 14, 1984, to Karen and Ed Zuckerberg. They lived in Dobbs Ferry, New York, with Mark's three sisters, Randi, Donna, and Arielle. His father is a dentist. His mother is a psychiatrist but has always helped out in her husband's dental office. Ed Zuckerberg computerized his dental practice the year after their son was born.

One year during their winter

Zuckerberg at Facebook's F8 conference

Atari
800

break from school, the Zuckerberg siblings decided to film a Star Wars parody they called Star Wars Sill-ogy. Each morning they had production meetings. Mark played Luke Skywalker, and his two-year-old sister walked around in a garbage can to play R2-D2. A few years later, Zuckerberg chose a Star Wars theme for his bar mitzvah.

Zuckerberg had been around high-tech toys and computers all his life. The family had an early personal computer—an Atari 800 that came with a disk that could be programmed. Zuckerberg's father taught him the Atari BASIC programming, and then turned it over to him to work on. Zuckerberg got a book about programming and mostly taught himself how to do it.

PRODIGY

Mark Zuckerberg received his own computer when he was in the sixth grade. About this time, Zuckerberg's parents hired David Newman, a software developer, to tutor him in computers. Newman quickly realized his young pupil was a computer genius. Next Zuckerberg enrolled in a graduate-level computer course at a local college. When his father took him to the first class, the teacher thought the boy was there to accompany his dad. Ed Zuckerberg explained that it was his young son who was the student.

By twelve, he was programming his computer, a Quantex 486DX that ran Windows 3.1. One of his projects was to create a network at the Zuckerberg home, which he called ZuckNet. He designed a program that would allow the family to send messages to one another from any computer in the house. It was also used to let his father know when his patients arrived at the dental office, located in the basement of their home. This was only the beginning of his projects.

He wrote programming for computer games—sometimes incorporating some art drawn by his friends. One game he designed was a version of Monopoly set in his middle school. Another was a game of Risk, which Zuckerberg explained was "centered around the ancient Roman Empire. You played against Julius Caesar. He was good, and I was never able to win." Zuckerberg was a good student at Ardsley High School, and especially excelled in math and science. But Ardsley did not have enough

Phillips Exeter Academy

high-level computer science and math courses, so he transferred to Phillips Exeter Academy in New Hampshire, a boarding school for high school students. Zuckerberg was drawn not only to Exeter's math and scince classes but also to its excellent Latin program.

When Zuckerberg arrived at Exeter, he received the Photo Address Book, which contained the photos, names, and addresses of students and faculty. The students called this book the facebook. This book helped him get to know his fellow students. It didn't take long for Zuckerberg to get settled into his new life at Exeter. He kept a busy schedule and was the captain of their fencing team, while keeping up a demanding academic schedule. He was a gifted student who could read and write French, Hebrew, Latin, and ancient Greek.

SYNAPSE

During his senior year, Zuckerberg and his buddies were sitting around discussing what they would choose as their topics for their independent projects. Zuckerberg was listening to a playlist of music on his computer, when suddenly it played the last song and it stopped. Zuckerberg thought his computer should know what he wanted to listen to next.

In response to that moment, he and his friend Adam D'Angelo designed a program that would consider the listener's musical taste, figure out the pattern of which songs you usually listened to around one another, and then choose a playlist that would match your preferences. He called the program Synapse. Zuckerberg posted a free version of it on the Internet.

Cocreator of Synapse, Adam D'Angelo.

Synapse was a hit. Not long after it was released, major companies including Microsoft and America Online approached the boys. Some companies offered to buy Synapse from them at first for one million dollars, then two million. Zuckerberg and D'Angelo decided not to sell it. Zuckerberg said, "I don't really like putting a price tag on the stuff I do. That's just . . . not the point."

By the time they went to college a few months later, they changed their minds and decided they should have sold Synapse after all. But by then the big companies no longer wanted to buy it. Zuckerberg realized they had been naïve

Harvard University

about Synapse. He learned that in the future he would need legal advice when it came to the products he developed.

Zuckerberg arrived at Harvard in the fall of 2002. He chose to begin working toward a double major, one in psychology and one in computer science. He joined Alpha Epsilon Pi, a Jewish fraternity. It was at one of their fraternity parties a year later

Zuckerberg with girlfriend, Priscilla Chan.

that Zuckerberg met his girlfriend, Priscilla Chan, while standing in line for the bathroom. Chan described him as "this nerdy guy who was just a little bit out there."

Zuckerberg admits that like a little kid, he gets bored easily, but computers were always exciting. Together these two realities gave Zuckerberg lots of ideas. While in college, he constantly created cool new computer programs. He would work on a program for hours. When it was done, he would show it to his friends, then move on to the next idea.

One program he created came from the idea that Harvard students would be interested to see which other students were enrolled in their classes. He designed a program to make it possible and called it CourseMatch.

FACEMASH FRENZY

During the last week of October 2003, his sophomore year, a friend gave him the idea for a program he called Facemash. Zuckerberg hacked into Harvard sites and retrieved photos of female students, then wrote an algorithm to run the program. When Facemash was ready, it would pull up photos of two girls side by side, and ask users to vote on which girl was the "hottest." He told a few friends about the site, and they told a few friends, and they told a few friends. Within four hours, more than 450 people visited the site and about 22,000 votes were placed. The guys at Harvard enjoyed making their "hottest" choices. The girls at Harvard were not happy about being judged on their looks. And Harvard's administration was unhappy with all of it. They disabled Zuckerberg's Internet connection.

Zuckerberg was brought in to the Administrative Board to discuss his actions. When it was over, he had not been suspended but was placed on probation. When the university newspaper, the *Harvard Crimson*, asked Zuckerberg about creating Facemash, he told them the part that interested him most was the programming that made it function.

Sometimes Zuckerberg and his friends (who called him Zuck) would get together at Pinocchio's, the local pizza joint, to talk about technology trends. He recalled how their conversations usually went: "We'd say, 'Isn't it obvious that everyone was going to be on the Internet? Isn't it, like, inevitable that there would be a huge social network of people?' It was something that we expected to happen."

About this time, senior students Divya Narendra and twins Cameron Winklevoss and Tyler Winklevoss asked Zuckerberg to help them with a website they were working

Divya Narendra and twins Cameron Winklevoss and Tyler Winklevoss.

on, which they called Harvard Connection (later called ConnectU). Zuckerberg was known as a programming prodigy, while the other three were not computer programmers. Zuckerberg informally worked on their project for a little while with no pay, then abandoned it altogether.

Instead, he began working on his next project—the one that would make him famous.

In late January 2004 Zuckerberg began writing a programming code. He was so immersed in his work that he didn't sleep. He didn't eat. He didn't talk to his friends. Just like Bill Gates had done in his Harvard dorm room almost exactly twenty-nine years before.

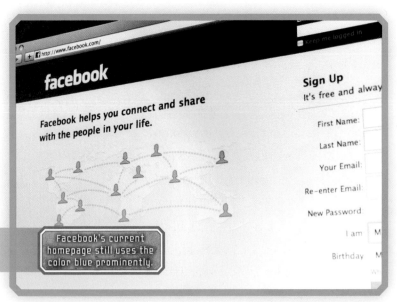

Facebook's current homepage still uses the color blue prominently.

THE FACEBOOK

It took him about a week to finish the program for the website he called thefacebook.com. The color blue used on the logo was Zuckerberg's choice. He is color-blind to red and green, so the color blue is the one he can see the best. Zuckerberg would later recall that he almost didn't launch the program, saying, "If I hadn't launched it that day, I was about to just can it and go on to the next thing I was about to do."

Eduardo Saverin

The site opened on February 4, 2004. Zuckerberg invited a few friends, and they invited a few friends, and they invited a few friends. With Facemash Zuckerberg had used photos without permission—but with the-facebook.com, users themselves would put up their own photos and personal information. Zuckerberg told his friend Eduardo Saverin, an economics major, about it. Saverin saw the possibilities and invested $1,000 toward start-up costs of the project. His friend Dustin

Dustin Moskovitz

Moskovitz helped with technical issues, and Chris Hughes became the spokesperson for thefacebook.com team. It was an instant success. In four days, there were more than 650 users at Harvard. After three weeks, Zuckerberg expanded it to include other large universities.

Only a few months after the launch of thefacebook.com, Zuckerberg moved operations to Silicon Valley. Moskovitz went to California with Zuckerberg, and Saverin went to New York in order to sell advertising. The house where they lived in Los Altos—which they called Casa Facebook— looked like a huge dorm room full of desks, computers,

Mark Zuckerberg and Chris Hughes at Harvard shortly after the launch of Facebook.

and food, with a wall spattered with green paintball shots. Also living in the house were Andrew McCollum and Sean Parker, the cofounder of Napster. Through the summer, they worked hard and played hard. Perhaps they played a little too hard since Zuckerberg got a complaint letter from the landlord asking them not to throw furniture into the pool, climb on the roof, or talk outside after ten P.M.

COURT CASE

On September 2, 2004, Divya Narendra, Cameron Winklevoss, and Tyler Winklevoss filed a lawsuit claiming Zuckerberg stole the source code, business model, and original idea from ConnectU. Suddenly Zuckerberg was faced with defending himself against their claim. He denied stealing anything from them. They were in a standoff.

In reality, the idea for a social network did not come from either side. Zuckerberg was influenced by the "facebook" Photo Address Book from his high school, Exeter. And Friendster, a social network on the Internet, was already being widely used. Only five days after Zuckerberg launched thefacebook.com, on February 9, 2004, an article appeared about it in the *Harvard Crimson*. In it Kevin Davis, director of residential computing, said that Harvard had been working toward creating a facebook of their own, and they intended to complete it by the end of the spring semester. Zuckerberg was quoted in the same article saying, "Everyone's been talking a lot about a universal facebook within Harvard. I think it's kind of silly that it would take the University a couple of years to get around to it. I can do it better than they can, and I can do it in a week."

Zuckerberg maintained that thefacebook.com and ConnectU were totally different—theirs focused on dating, his on networking. The legal fees to fight the lawsuit would cost $20,000 a month. Ultimately, the lawsuit was set-tled for $65 million in a combination of cash and stocks.

Screenshot of Zuckerberg's own Facebook profile.

(After this original settlement, the Winklevoss twins took Zuckerberg back to court, claiming they were misled. In the spring of 2011, a court of appeals ruled in the case. The judge rejected the claim of the Winklevoss twins, and said the time had come for litigation on the issue to be finished.)

By December 2004 thefacebook.com was being used at hundreds of American college campuses and had nearly one million users. By the next year, it was in high schools and schools in foreign countries. In May 2005, they also raised $12.7 million through an investor. In August 2005 Zuckerberg officially changed the name from thefacebook. com to just Facebook. Their mission was to give people the ability to share and make the world more connected.

Facebook was a huge hit. Once again major companies approached Zuckerberg to buy his company. Yahoo! offered to buy Facebook for $1 billion. Zuckerberg's longtime girl-friend, Priscilla Chan, who is in medical school, remembered this period of time being stressful for him. No doubt he took into consideration his previous experience when he chose not to sell Synapse for a lot of money when he could have.

In the end, Zuckerberg decided not to sell Facebook. He felt that anyone could make a lot of money, but not everyone could have a social network. Zuckerberg said, "It's not about the price. This is my baby, and I want to keep running it, I want to keep growing it."

ANOTHER ONE LEAVES HARVARD

By 2004, Zuckerberg decided to leave Harvard to devote himself full time to his company—like Bill Gates had done twenty-nine years before. Within the next year, he sought out smart, young engineers and computer programmers who were just out of college to work at Facebook. By the close of 2005, Facebook had 5.5 million users.

Sheryl Sandberg

Like Google, Facebook provides its employees with perks, like three meals a day and snacks for free—along with dry cleaning. And like Google, their profits come from advertising. Sheryl Sandberg, who previously worked at Google, is the current chief operating officer who oversees advertising. In some ways,

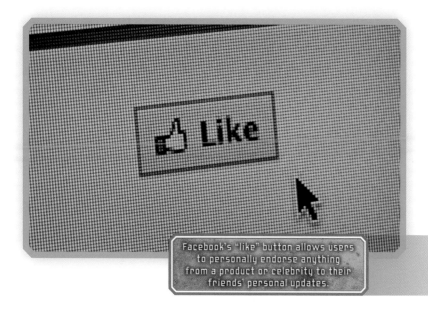

Facebook's "like" button allows users to personally endorse anything from a product or celebrity to their friends' personal updates.

Facebook can tailor advertising even more specifically than Google can, because users' profiles clearly state their interests. If a user "likes" an advertisement it is like a personal endorsement. To have a friend recommend a product is the best way to market any product—and that is exactly what users do on Facebook. So along with more and more users each day, Facebook also gathers more and more money from companies who advertise their products.

As the popularity of Facebook took off, the site hit 100 million users in 2008. They had a toga party to celebrate the milestone. By December 2009 Facebook had 350 million users. The company grew so fast that each time they moved into new offices, they quickly outgrew the space and had to move again. Facebook plans to move in the near future to Menlo Park, but their current location, which Zuckerberg calls the Bunker, has high ceilings, concrete floors, and big windows. The halls have RipStiks (similar to skateboards) lined up for anyone who wants to ride them. Zuckerberg does not have an office—and no one else does either. It is just an open space filled with lots of office furniture. There is a conference room called the Aquarium in the middle of the workspace, which has glass walls on three sides so everyone can see in. Instead of taking Facebook public, Zuckerberg has kept it as a private company with control over it himself. Facebook has more than two thousand employees and has offices all over the world.

FAME, FORTUNE, AND CHARITY

Zuckerberg has become as famous as Facebook, but he doesn't like it when the focus is all about him. In 2010 he was chosen as *Time* magazine's Person of the Year. When Zuckerberg told his father that he would be featured on the cover of *Time* magazine, he added that it must have been a slow year.

Being in the public eye isn't always easy for Zuckerberg,

known for wearing jeans, sneakers, T-shirts, and hoodies. Some people feel that it's hard to have a conversation with him. Lev Grossman, the reporter who wrote the Person of the Year cover story for *Time* magazine, wrote that Zuckerberg "approaches conversation as a way of exchanging data as rapidly and efficiently as possible . . .

Person *of the* Year

Facebook's
Mark
Zuckerberg
THE CONNECTOR

Zuckerberg's *Time* magazine cover.

and if he has no data to transmit, he abruptly falls silent." Yet, he has a calm way about him, a warm smile, and an easy laugh. His friends know Zuck to be a sympathetic listener to their problems. Zuckerberg's mother says being raised with three sisters taught him to have a sensitive side.

Also in 2010, *Vanity Fair* magazine chose Mark Zuckerberg as number one on their list of the one hundred most influential people (number two was Steve Jobs; number three was Larry Page and Sergey Brin; number five was Jeff Bezos). They wrote, "This year *Vanity Fair* anoints Zuck as our new Caesar. He rules from the imperial capital of Palo Alto, California, the Rome of our nascent millennium." It seems Zuckerberg has come full circle—when he created his version of Risk when he was a kid, he played against Julius Caesar but couldn't beat him. Now, according to *Vanity Fair*, Zuckerberg has finally triumphed over Caesar.

Today Facebook has been embraced by people of all ages, from teens to grandparents. As of July 2011, Facebook had 750 million users. About 33 percent of all Americans have a Facebook account, 70 percent of its users live outside the United States. One out of every thirteen people in the entire world has a Facebook account. Each day around 700,000 new people join its membership.

Even though Zuckerberg is currently worth more than $13.5 billion, he lives modestly. He does not own a TV, and the car he drives is an Acura. For years he rented a house near the Facebook office. In May 2011 Zuckerberg bought his first home. Even though he paid $7 million for the five-thousand-square-foot house, it is a modest choice for a man with so much wealth.

Even though Zuckerberg is not extravagant in the way he lives, he is extravagant in the way he gives. After hearing the school system in Newark, New Jersey, was having problems, Zuckerberg announced he would donate assets worth $100 million to them. Mark Zuckerberg, the youngest of the tech titans, has joined Bill Gates, one of the oldest of the titans, in the Giving Pledge—a commitment to give away much of his wealth to charity during his lifetime or after his death. Zuckerberg said, "People wait until late in their career to give back. But why wait when there is so much to be done?"

CONCLUSION

WHEN BILL GATES WAS A TEEN, he dreamed that someday there would be a computer on every desk and in every home. His dream has nearly come true. According to Gartner, Inc., an information research company, there are currently more than one billion personal computers worldwide. They estimate that by 2014 the number of PCs will be two billion.

These modern tech titans—Bill Gates, Steve Jobs, Jeff Bezos, Sergey Brin, Larry Page, and Mark Zuckerberg— each began their career by being interested in computers. Each of them brought their own individual skills and innovations to the world of computing. Each of them has changed the way we communicate and live our lives.

Today the next generation of tech titans is sitting in classrooms all over the world. Who knows, maybe the next great idea—the next huge jump in human communication— is stirring in someone's imagination right now.

Bill Gates

Jeff Bezos

Steve Jobs

Larry Page

Sergey Brin

Mark Zuckerberg

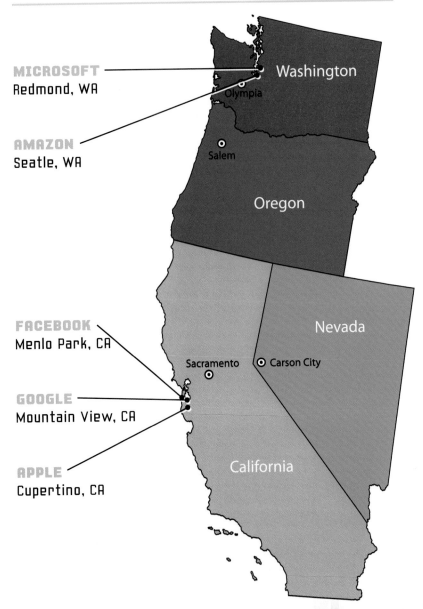

MICROSOFT
Redmond, WA

Washington

Olympia

AMAZON
Seatle, WA

Salem

Oregon

Nevada

FACEBOOK
Menlo Park, CA

Sacramento

Carson City

GOOGLE
Mountain View, CA

APPLE
Cupertino, CA

California

TIMELINE

- **1975:** Microsoft founded

- **1976:** Apple Computers established

- **1981:** Microsoft introduces personal computer

- **1995:** Amazon opens for business

- **1996:** Page and Brin create Backrub search engine

- **1997** Backrub renamed Google

- **1998:** Google Inc. comes into existence; iMac unveiled

- **2001:** Apple releases iPod; Microsoft launches Xbox

- **2003:** Zuckerberg launches Facemash

- **2004:** TheFacebook.com opens

- **2007:** Amazon's Kindle released

- **2008:** Facebook gets 100 million users; Google Chrome launches

- **2010:** Apple introduces the iPad

- **2012:** Apples iPhone 5 schedules release

BOOKS

Gates, Bill. *The Road Ahead*. New York, New York:
   Penguin, 1995.

Imbimbo, Anthony. *Steve Jobs: The Brilliant Mind
   Behind Apple*. Pleasantville, New York: Gareth Stevens
   Publishing, 2009.

Sherman, Josepha. *Jeff Bezos: King of Amazon*. Brookfield,
   Conneticut: Twenty-First Century Books, 2001.

Vise, David, and Mark Malseed. *The Google Story*. New
   York, New York: Delacorte Press, 2005.

Young, Jeffrey S., and William L. Simon. *iCon*. Hoboken,
   New Jersey: John Wiley & Sons, 2005.

ARTICLES

"A Conversation with Amazon.com CEO Jeff Bezos." *Charlie
   Rose Show*, February 19, 2007. http://www.charlierose.
   com/view/interview/8784.

Allison, David. "Transcript of a Video History Interview
   with Mr. William "Bill" Gates." *Bill Gates Interview,
   Winner of the 1993 Price Waterhouse Leadership Award
   for Lifetime Achievement, Computerworld Smithsonian
   Awards*. National Museum of American History,
   Smithsonian Institute, 1993.

Gates, Bill. *2011 Annual Letter from Bill Gates*, 2011.
   http://www.gatesfoundation.org/annual-letter/2011/
   Documents/2011-annual-letter.pdf.

Gates, Bill, and Melinda Gates. *Pledge letters*, 2010. http://
   givingpledge.org/Content/media/PledgeLetters.pdf.

Gates, William H. "Raising Bill Gates." *CNNMoney*, May 1,
   2009.

Goodell, Jeff. "Bill Gates." *Rolling Stone*, November 15,
   2007: 170-173.

Grossman, Lev. "Bill Gates Goes Back to School." *Time*,
   June 18, 2007.

Grynbaum, Michael. *Mark E. Zuckerberg '06: The whiz
   behind thefacebook.com*, June 10, 2004. http://www
   .thecrimson.com/article/2004/6/10/mark-e-zuckerberg
   -06-the-whiz/.

Helft, Miguel. *Google Founders' Ultimate Perk: A NASA
   Runway*, September 13, 2007. www.newyorktimes.com
   (accessed April 15, 2011).

Hertzfeld, Andy. *Folklore*, February 1981. http://folklore
   .org/StoryView.py?project=Macintosh&story=Reality
   _Distortion_Field.txt&sortOrder=SortbyDate.

Ignatius, Adi. "Meet the Google Guys." *Time*, February 12,
   2006.

"In Search of the Real Google." *Time*, February 12, 2006.

"Inspiring Interview with Larry Page, Founder of Google."
    January 18, 2009. http://changeminds.wordpress
    .com/2009/01/18/inspiring-interview-with-larry-page
    -founder-of-google/.

Issacson, Walter. "In Search of the Real Bill Gates." *Time*,
    January 13, 1997: 44.

"Jeff Bezos Interview." *Academy of Achievement*, May
    4, 2001. http://www.achievement.org/autodoc/page/
    bez0int-1.

Jennings, Peter. "Persons of the Week: Lary Page and
    Sergey Brin." February 20, 2004. http://abcnews.go.com/
    WNT/PersonOfWeek/story?id=131833&page=1.

Jobs, Steve. "Commencement address at Stanford
    University." *Stanford University News*, June 12, 2005.
    http://news.stanford.edu/news/2005/june15/jobs-061505
    .html

Kahney, Leander. *John Sculley on Steve Jobs, The Full
    Interview Transcript*, October 14, 2010. http://www
    .cultofmac.com/john-sculley-on-steve-jobs-the-full
    -interview-transcript/63295/comment-page-1 (accessed
    March 15, 2011).

Krantz, Michael, David S. Jackson, Janice Maloney, and
    Cathy Booth. "Steve's Two Jobs." *Time*, October 18,
    1999: 62.

Levy, Steven. "The Future of Reading." *Newsweek*,
   November 7, 2007.

Moritz, Michael. "The Updated Book off Jobs." *Time*,
   January 3, 1983.

Morrow, Daniel. "Transcript of interview with Steve Jobs."
   *Steve Jobs, Smithsonian Institution Oral and Video
   Histories*, April 20, 1995.

"NASA." *NASA Press Release*, February 1, 2010. http://
   www.nasa.gov/home/hqnews/2010/feb/HQ_C10-004
   _Commercia_Crew_Dev.html.

Quittner, Joshua. "Jeff Bezos: Bio: An Eye On the Future."
   Time, December 7, 1999.

Sewer, Andy. "Gates on Gates." *Fortune International
   (Asia)*, July 6, 2009: 40–40.

"Tales of a Real-Life Zuckerberg." Dealbook, *New York
   Times*, September 13, 2010.

Williams, Gregg, and Rob Moore. "The Apple Story."
   Apple History, December 1984. http://apple2history.org/
   museum/artuckes/byte8412/.

Wilson, Lyzette. "One on One with Larry Page, CEO of
   Google." *TechBiz*, August 5, 2001. http://www.biz
   journals.com/sanfrancisco/stories/2001/08/06/
   newscolumn8.html.

"Zuckerberg Dad: Mark Got Computer Exposure Young."
    Associated Press. February 5, 2011. http://www.sun
    times.com/lifestyles/3682480-423/zuckerberg-mark
    -certain-early-son.html.

WEBSITES

http://blueorigin.com/nsresearch.html

http://www.google.com/corporate/history.html

http://www.google.com/corporate/tenthings.html

http://www.exeter.edu/admissions/109_1220.aspx

http://www.microsoft.com/about/en/us/default.aspx

INDEX

ALSO AVAILABLE

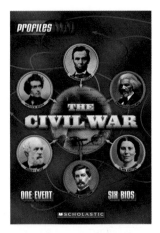

PROFILES: THE CIVIL WAR
978-0-545-23756-7

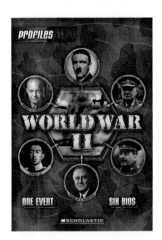

PROFILES: WORLD WAR II
978-0-545-31655-2